First World War
and Army of Occupation
War Diary
France, Belgium and Germany

14 DIVISION
Headquarters, Branches and Services
Royal Army Ordnance Corps
Deputy Assistant Director Ordnance Services
9 May 1915 - 31 May 1919

WO95/1885/1

The Naval & Military Press Ltd
www.nmarchive.com
Published in association with The National Archives

Published by

The Naval & Military Press Ltd

Unit 10 Ridgewood Industrial Park,
Uckfield, East Sussex,
TN22 5QE England
Tel: +44 (0) 1825 749494

www.naval-military-press.com
www.nmarchive.com

This diary has been reprinted in facsimile from the original. Any imperfections are inevitably reproduced and the quality may fall short of modern type and cartographic standards.

© **Crown Copyright**
Images reproduced by permission of The National Archives, London, England, 2015.

Contents

Document type	Place/Title	Date From	Date To
Heading	WO95/1885 1915 May-May 1919		
Heading	14th Division D.A.D.O.S. May 1915-May 1919		
Heading	14th Division (D.A.D.O.S.) Vol. I May-1915-May 1919		
Heading	War Diary of D.A.D.O.S. 14th Division From 9-5-15 To 30-6-15		
War Diary	Aldershot	09/05/1915	11/05/1915
War Diary	Boulogne St Omer	11/05/1915	16/05/1915
War Diary	St Omer	17/05/1915	20/05/1915
War Diary	Watten	21/05/1915	27/05/1915
War Diary	Steenworde	28/05/1915	30/05/1915
War Diary	Westoutre	31/05/1915	10/06/1915
War Diary	N. Watou	14/06/1915	21/06/1915
War Diary	Nr Vlamertinghe	22/06/1915	30/06/1915
Heading	D.A.D.O.S. 14th Division Vol. II		
Heading	War Diary Of D.A.D.O.S. 14th Division from 1.7.15 to 31.7.15		
War Diary	N. Vlamertinghe	01/07/1915	31/07/1915
Heading	Headquarters 14th Division D.A.D.O.S. Vol. III From 1-31.8.15		
Heading	War Diary of Major Williams-Freeman, D.A.D.O.S. 14th Division From Aug 1st /15 To August 31st /15		
War Diary	N. Vlamertinghe	01/08/1915	31/08/1915
Heading	H.Q. 14th Division D.A.D.O.S. Vol. IX Sep 1 15		
Miscellaneous	Enclosure To 121/6607	17/09/1915	17/09/1915
Heading	War Diary of Major A. Williams Freeman D.A.D.O.S. 14th Division from 1st Sept. 1915 to 30 Sept. 1916		
War Diary	N. Vlamertinghe	02/09/1915	30/09/1915
Heading	H.Q. 14th Div. D.A.D.O.S. Vol. 5 Oct. 15		
Heading	War Diary Of D.A.D.O.S. 14th Division 1-10-15 To 31-10-15		
Heading	War Diary Of Major A P William Freeman D.A.D.O.S. 14th Division from 1st Oct 1915 to 31st Oct 1915		
War Diary	N. Vlamertinghe	01/10/1915	31/10/1915
Heading	H.Q. 14th Division D.A.D.O.S. Vol. 6 Nov 15		
Heading	War Diary Of D.A.D.O.S. 14th (Light) Division from Nov 1st 1915 to Nov. 30th 1915		
War Diary	N. Vlamertinghe	01/11/1915	29/11/1915
Heading	D.A.D.O.S. 14th Div. Vol. 7 Dec. 1915		
War Diary	N. Vlamertinghe	06/12/1915	31/12/1915
Heading	D.A.D.O.S. 14th Div. Vol. 8 Jan. 1916		
Heading	War Diary Of D.A.D.O.S. 14th Division 1st January to 31st January 1916		
War Diary	Vlamertinghe	01/01/1916	31/01/1916
Heading	War Diary D.A.D.O.S. 14th Division 1st February To 29th February 1916		
War Diary	Vlamertinghe	01/02/1916	13/02/1916
War Diary	Esquilbec	13/02/1916	18/02/1916
War Diary	Flessels	19/02/1916	23/02/1916
War Diary	Doullens	24/02/1916	25/02/1916

War Diary	Sus St. Leger	26/02/1916	29/02/1916
Heading	War Diary D.A.D.O.S. 14th Division For March 1916 Mar 1st-Mar 31st vol 10		
War Diary	Barly	01/03/1916	04/03/1916
War Diary	Berneville	05/03/1916	15/03/1916
War Diary	Warlus	16/03/1916	31/03/1916
Heading	War Diary April 1st-April 30th 1916 D.A.D.O.S. 14th Div Vol 11		
War Diary	Warlus	01/04/1916	30/04/1916
Heading	War Diary May 1st-31st 1916 D.A.D.O.S. 14 Div. Vol 12		
War Diary	Warlus	01/05/1916	31/05/1916
Heading	War Diary June 1st-June 30th 1916 D.A.D.O.S. 14 Div Vol 13		
War Diary	Warlus	01/06/1916	30/06/1916
Heading	War Diary D.A.D.O.S. 14 Div. July 1st-31st 1916 Vol 14		
War Diary	Warlus	01/07/1916	31/07/1916
Heading	War Diary D.A.D.O.S. 14 Div. August 1st To August 31st 1916 Vol 15		
War Diary	Frouen Le Grand	01/08/1916	01/08/1916
War Diary	Berneville	02/08/1916	06/08/1916
War Diary	Buire	07/08/1916	12/08/1916
War Diary	Albert	13/08/1916	31/08/1916
Heading	War Diary D.A.D.O.S. 14 Div. Sept 1 1916 Sept 30 1916 Vol 16		
War Diary	Belloy S Leonard	01/09/1916	05/09/1916
War Diary	Belloy	06/09/1916	11/09/1916
War Diary	Buire	12/09/1916	21/09/1916
War Diary	Le Cauroy	22/09/1916	28/09/1916
War Diary	Warlus	29/09/1916	30/09/1916
Heading	War Diary D.A.D.O.S. 14th Div. Oct. 1st-Oct 31st 1916 Vol 17		
War Diary	Warlus	01/10/1916	26/10/1916
War Diary	Le Cauroy	27/10/1916	31/10/1916
Heading	War Diary D.A.D.O.S. 14 Div. Nov 1 30 1916 Vol 18		
War Diary	Le Cauroy	01/11/1916	30/11/1916
Heading	War Diary Of D.A.D.O.S. 14th Division From 1-12-16 To 31-12-16 Vol 19		
War Diary	Le Cauroy	01/12/1916	18/12/1916
War Diary	Warlus	19/12/1916	31/12/1916
Miscellaneous	Jan. 1917		
War Diary	Warlus	01/01/1917	31/01/1917
Heading	War Diary D.A.D.O.S. 14 Div. From February 1st 1917 To February 28th 1917 Vol 21		
War Diary	Warlus	01/02/1917	28/02/1917
Heading	War Diary D.A.D.O.S. 14 Div. From Mar 1st 1917 To Mar 31st 1917 Vol. 22		
War Diary	Warlus	01/03/1917	31/03/1917
Heading	War Diary D.A.D.O.S. 14 Div. April 1st-30th 1917 Vol 23		
War Diary	Warlus	01/04/1917	26/04/1917
War Diary	Arras	27/04/1917	30/04/1917
Heading	War Diary May 1st To May 31st 1917 D.A.D.O.S. 14 Div Vol 24		
War Diary	Arras	01/05/1917	15/05/1917

War Diary	M.17. C Central Sheet 57C.	16/05/1917	21/05/1917
War Diary	M 17 C Central	22/05/1917	31/05/1917
Heading	War Diary D.A.D.O.S. 14 Div. June 1st-June 30 1917 Vol 25		
War Diary	M 17 C	01/06/1917	07/06/1917
War Diary	M 17 C Central Sheet 57 C.	08/06/1917	10/06/1917
War Diary	Marieux	11/06/1917	30/06/1917
Heading	War Diary July 1st-1917 To July 31st 1917 D.A.D.O.S. 14 Div. Vol 26		
War Diary	Marilux	01/07/1917	11/07/1917
War Diary	S. Jans Cappel	12/07/1917	31/07/1917
Heading	War Diary D.A.D.O.S. 14 Div. Aug 1st-Aug 31st 1917 Vol 27		
War Diary	S. Jan. Cappel	01/08/1917	07/08/1917
War Diary	Caestre	08/08/1917	16/08/1917
War Diary	Reninghelst	17/08/1917	31/08/1917
Heading	War Diary Sept. 1st-1917 To Sept. 30 1917 D.A.D.O.S. 14 Division Vol 28		
War Diary	Berthen	01/09/1917	02/09/1917
War Diary	N. Eglise	03/09/1917	30/09/1917
Heading	War Diary D.A.D.O.S. 14 Div. Oct. 1st-Oct. 31st 1917 Vol 29		
War Diary	Ravelsberg	01/10/1917	08/10/1917
War Diary	Westoutre	09/10/1917	11/10/1917
War Diary	La Clyte	12/10/1917	24/10/1917
War Diary	Berthen	25/10/1917	31/10/1917
Heading	D.A.D.O.S. 14 Div. War Diary Nov. 1st 1917 To Nov. 30th 1917 Vol 30		
War Diary	Berthen	01/11/1917	11/11/1917
War Diary	Wizernes	12/11/1917	30/11/1917
Heading	War Diary D.A.D.O.S. 14 Div. Vol 31		
War Diary	Wizernes	01/12/1917	03/12/1917
War Diary	Vlamertinghe	04/12/1917	07/12/1917
War Diary	Vlam	08/12/1917	12/12/1917
War Diary	Vlamertinghe	13/12/1917	26/12/1917
War Diary	Wizerne	27/12/1917	31/12/1917
Miscellaneous	Jan 1918		
War Diary	Wizernes	01/01/1918	04/01/1918
War Diary	Mericourt	05/01/1918	24/01/1918
War Diary	Flavy	24/01/1918	28/01/1918
War Diary	Jussy	30/01/1918	31/01/1918
Heading	War Diary of D.A.D.O.S. February 1918 Vol 33		
War Diary	Jussy	01/02/1918	28/02/1918
Heading	War Diary D.A.D.O.S. 14 Div Mar 1st-31st 1918 Vol 34		
War Diary	Jussy	01/03/1918	22/03/1918
War Diary	Beaumont	22/03/1918	22/03/1918
War Diary	Guiscard	23/03/1918	23/03/1918
War Diary	Noyon	24/03/1918	24/03/1918
War Diary	Lassingy	25/03/1918	25/03/1918
War Diary	Estrees St. Dennis	26/03/1918	31/03/1918
Heading	War Diary D.A.D.O.S. 14 Div. April 1st-30th 1918 Vol 35		
War Diary	Hibercourt	01/04/1918	03/04/1918
War Diary	Saleux	04/04/1918	11/04/1918
War Diary	Hucqueliers	12/04/1918	15/04/1918

War Diary	Ecquedecques	16/04/1918	21/04/1918
War Diary	Coyecques	22/04/1918	29/04/1918
War Diary	Torcy	30/04/1918	30/04/1918
Heading	May 1918 D.A.D.O.S.		
War Diary	Torcy	01/05/1918	09/05/1918
War Diary	S Quentin	10/05/1918	31/05/1918
Heading	War Diary June 1/16 1918 H Leonard Robuls Hut D.A.D.O.S. 14th Division Vol 37		
War Diary	S Quentin	01/06/1918	16/06/1918
Heading	War Diary D.A.D.O.S. 14 Division 4th/22nd July 1918 Vol 24		
War Diary	Wierre Effroy	04/07/1918	12/07/1918
War Diary	Eperlecques	13/07/1918	22/07/1918
War Diary	In The Field	24/07/1918	31/07/1918
War Diary	Dannes	23/07/1918	23/07/1918
War Diary	Eperlecques	07/08/1918	13/08/1918
War Diary	Proven	20/08/1918	23/08/1918
War Diary	In The Field	01/09/1918	31/05/1919

Woods 1885
1915 June – June 1916

14TH DIVISION

D. A. D. O. S.
MAY 1915 – MAY 1919

14th Division

14th Division (D.A. DOS.)

Vol. I.

Nov '15 —
May '19

Army Form C. 2118.

WAR DIARY
INTELLIGENCE SUMMARY
(Erase heading not required.)

Instructions regarding War Diaries and Intelligence Summaries are contained in F.S. Regs., Part II. and the Staff Manual respectively. Title pages will be prepared in manuscript.

Hour, Date, Place	Summary of Events and Information	Remarks and references to Appendices
	Confidential War Diary of D.A.D.O.S. 14th Division From: 9 - 5 - 15. To 30 - 6 - 15.	

Army Form C. 2118.

WAR DIARY
or
INTELLIGENCE SUMMARY.
(Erase heading not required.)

Instructions regarding War Diaries and Intelligence Summaries are contained in F. S. Regs., Part II. and the Staff Manual respectively. Title pages will be prepared in manuscript.

Place	Date 1915 May	Hour	Summary of Events and Information	Remarks and references to Appendices
Aldershot	9th		Received orders on this day to proceed with Advanced Party of 14th Light Division on 11th instant to Folkestone travelling by Motor	
"	11		Left Aldershot at 6.30am & arrived at Folkestone 12.30pm Embarked at 4pm. & arrived Boulogne 5.30pm. Remained night at Boulogne	
Boulogne St Omer		10am	Left by Motor & arrived at G.H.Q. at 1pm. Reported myself to D.D.O.S. G.H.Q. who instructed me to come & see him on any points I wished to raise	
"	13 to 15		Inspected the area allotted to Division in conjunction with Senior Supply Officer & decided provisionally on position of Refilling Points.	
"	16		The area allotted to Division slightly altered & it was therefore necessary to select other refilling points which I did with C.S.O.	

Army Form C. 2118.

WAR DIARY
or
INTELLIGENCE SUMMARY.
(Erase heading not required.)

Place	Date 1915 May	Hour	Summary of Events and Information	Remarks and references to Appendices
St Omer	17		Took over from 3 Ton Lorries from 14th Div. Supply Column. Received from D.D.S. G.H.Q. 1000 respirators with instructions to issue to Infantry, Cavalry, R.A. & R.E.	
"	18		Inspected Area allotted to Division & decided that Brigade Warrant Officers G.O.C. & Staff should remain with their Brigade Hd. Qrs. in the future & that Lorries should proceed to Refilling Points daily with stores.	
	19		Took over from I.S.O.S. G.H.Q. 1000 smoke Helmets with instructions to issue 50 to each Infantry Battn. & 10 to Cav. & R.E. & 5 to each Battery R.F.A. for Training Officers.	
	20		Proceeded to WATTEN when the Division commenced to detrain.	

WAR DIARY
or
INTELLIGENCE SUMMARY.

Army Form C. 2118.

Place	Date	Hour	Summary of Events and Information	Remarks and references to Appendices
WOTTEN	1915 May 21		Issued deficiencies & boots. Helmets so far as possible. Most of the units can strength recruit an issue of deficiencies before leaving England. Although no stores are arriving at Railhead yet I am urging that all lorries are to proceed to Refilling point daily & prior to Railhead to join the A.S.C. Staff, an idea of the method to be adopted.	
"	22		Statement continued. Visited Refilling Point of 4th Infantry Brigade & saw Brigade Staff.	
"	23		Statement continued. Visited 4 2" btty. Bde. Hol. Arc. & saw sub Condr. Lilly & Staff. He knows Lanid division man. I left England & is an old A.S.C. man. Report to Ordnance Commissioners that establishment of Travelling Kitchens complete.	
"	24		Statement continued. Visited R.A. Hob. Arc & Cyclist Company.	

WAR DIARY
or
INTELLIGENCE SUMMARY.
(Erase heading not required.)

Army Form C. 2118.

Place	Date	Hour	Summary of Events and Information	Remarks and references to Appendices
WATTEN	1916 May 25		Detachment continued. Instructions received that all woolen drawers, vests, body bands & blankets were to be returned. Issued orders accordingly & arranged lorries to remove from Refilling Points tomorrow. Also arranged for necessary Trucks.	
"	26		Proceeded to Railhead & superintended loading up of warm clothing and Blankets. Found that Hve Bethune had retained Cwt Cwb instead of Blankets. Reported to D.D. who directed that this unit might return their Great Coats. Trucks dispatched to Paris.	
"	27		Instructions received that a Reserve of Boots of 1000 refrictions to be maintained. Demanded accordingly on Base. Received 2000 from D.A.D. O.H.A.	

WAR DIARY
or
INTELLIGENCE SUMMARY

Army Form C. 2118.

Place	Date	Hour	Summary of Events and Information	Remarks and references to Appendices
Steenwoorde	1915 May 28		Divisional Head Quarters moved to Steenwoorde. Railhead at EBLINGHEM. Stores are now beginning to arrive from the Base & I find that the continued changing of units refilling Points owing to the movement of troops is trying my Staff rather high. In great difficulty in keeping the Brigade Staff with Brigade Hd Qrs. so that the members of that Staff who come to railhead after refilling may return to Brigade Hd Quart to rejoin their Hd Qrs. I wrote velre be from in army I.C. An alteration is to put Brigade Staff, with the Supply Column so that the men who proceeds to refilling point may travel in his lorry. I may have an opportunity of trying this.	
	29		Instructions received that no one will be allowed to Inft. Cav. R.A R.E. & R.A.M.C & that a divisional down I.J.S.O. to be maintained. Demanded accordingly in response to enquiry from I.J.S.J. 2nd Army replied that no	

WAR DIARY
or
INTELLIGENCE SUMMARY

Army Form C. 2118.

Place	Date 1915	Hour	Summary of Events and Information	Remarks and references to Appendices
Steenwerck	May 29		Lun Valley Travelling Kitchens in Avenswan.	
	30		Instructions received that Divl. Hd. Qrs. to move to WESTOUTRE tomorrow. Proceeded him & took over Offices & dump from J.A.S.T. 3rd Division. Own Infantry Brigades & remnt. of 14D replenished each.	
Westoutre	31		Moved to WESTOUTRE. Division now fairly concentrated. Decided therefore that it was better for units to come to Dump to draw Stores. Issued orders accordingly.	
	June 1st		Visited units of 8 & 3" bnty. Bde. Orders received to replace Swiss smock Helmets by Rectorials	
	2		System of units drawing stores at Dump working very smoothly. Stores coming up regularly.	

Army Form C. 2118.

WAR DIARY
or
INTELLIGENCE SUMMARY.
(Erase heading not required.)

Instructions regarding War Diaries and Intelligence Summaries are contained in F. S. Regs., Part II. and the Staff Manual respectively. Title pages will be prepared in manuscript.

Place	Date	Hour	Summary of Events and Information	Remarks and references to Appendices
Westoutre	1917 Janry 3.		Railhead now at CAISTRE. 14" Heavy Battery came under 2nd Corps & Ordnance Rifles.	
"	5		Tent about H/M damaged in a gale. Two Field Kitchens reported with broken axles. Arranged to remove them to Railhead & despatched to base.	
"	6		Received & landed over 20 Vermorel Sprayers to 85" Inft. Bde. First carts arrived for 3 Australians who returned them in lieu of Blanketts. Everything going smoothly & stores arriving regularly.	
"	7		Water Cart March V are showing signs of giving trouble. Design is for too heavy traffic for bad roads. Chief weakness is in clarifying cylinders which through continued vibration tear away from body of tank. Put in indent that stores you what no authority exists must not be indented for.	

1577 Wt. W10791/1773 500,000 1/15 D. D. & L.   A.D.S.S./Forms/C. 2118.

WAR DIARY or INTELLIGENCE SUMMARY

Army Form C. 2118.

Place	Date	Hour	Summary of Events and Information	Remarks and references to Appendices
Westoutre	1918 June 10.		Information received that all Infantry, Cav. R.A. R.E. & R.A.M.C. to have no respirators & one 2nd Pattern Helmet per man & a similar number returned to be filled. Travelling Kitchen with broken axle.	
Nr Watou	14.		Divisional Head Quarters moved to near WATOU. As divisions two were given trains very restricted owing to Jerry jump at Railhead that A.O.T. staff should go there & men with supply Column, remainder shifted stores to CAISTRE but left my Office with Head Quarters. The system of orderwise supply I now decide to adopt is that the men lorries proceed to the farm distilling spirits respectively land our stores & empty return to Railhead when they clear the trucks & the stores to the dump. The stores to be later put sent along are then sorted & laid out & placed in the respective lorries, staff then move up in clouds &c. Seems simple but I have my doubts.	

1577 Wt. W10791/1773 500,000 1/15 D.D. & L. A.D.S.S./Forms/C. 2118.

Army Form C. 2118.

WAR DIARY
or
INTELLIGENCE SUMMARY.
(Erase heading not required.)

Place	Date	Hour	Summary of Events and Information	Remarks and references to Appendices
2' Watson Southampton	1916 June 16		Instructions received that issue of Smoke Helmets is to be four per man disposed as follows:- Two with the man, one in divisional reserve & one in Corps & Army reserve.	
"	17		Supply Column transferred to Ordnance supplies to Supply Park. I find that the system adopted on the L. of C. is not working as well as could be wished. The main reason for this appears to be that out Refilling points, it is difficult to hold sufficient representatives of the consignees, & that lorries are sometimes delayed for four or five hours with the result they do not return to Railhead in time to be unloaded & tents erected ere in two o'clock. It is late in the evening before next day's stores are load out & loaded up, the men are usually tired & as a result the efforts of making up loads, estimating bulk requirements re outfits, will practically will, by causing too men immediately I believe will be many on the on our would be the best system to adopt. Another system returned to Sam with Britten amb.	

Army Form C. 2118.

WAR DIARY
or
INTELLIGENCE SUMMARY.
(Erase heading not required.)

Place	Date	Hour	Summary of Events and Information	Remarks and references to Appendices
R. Waton	1916 Sept. 19		Arrived order published that windows & roofs of Helmets should be protected by a stout piece of cardboard in wood.	
"	21.		Orders received for Administration offices to move up to Advanced Area tomorrow. In conjunction with Town Major selected good Dump in Poperinghe.	
A.Wemerlinghe	22		Moved up to Advanced Area & shifted Dump from Cassire to Poperinghe. Reported to Cdre. 2nd Army that sufficient Smoke Helmets received to equip to men, but that owing to many breakages it had not been possible to do so.	
"	23		Issued 25% of Blankets to Troops for Shelters. Water Carts fitted a lot of tanks. I.O.M. is fitting off foot Clarify up Cylinders & fitting up in front of tank & running the foot gear to back of tank. This looks as if it will work well	

Place	Date	Hour	Summary of Events and Information	Remarks and references to Appendices
Vlamertinghe	1917 June 24		Work going smoothly at dump & units drawing stores regularly	
"	25		Rifles & Bayonets I think I Motor Car & I m drivr pr lorry to be returned. Two yellow Machine Guns recvd from 5th Division & handed over to 6th Division L.I. Deficient of many spare parts. The Divisionals have now two Machine Guns. Genl ordered Baths started at Poperinghe. Instructed to hand over to Baths as early as possible. 4000 shirts, 4000 pairs of socks, 4000 towels to give them a stock sufficient for limited numbers.	
"	26		Confirmed that no indents to spare parts I [illegible] received from so & Division outstanding (except to Vickers & Co.) & indents in Base to replace. Complited certain unit in Lewis Hilants.	
"	27		Demanded our Vickers Machine Gun pr & Motor Machine Gun	

WAR DIARY

or
INTELLIGENCE SUMMARY

(Erase heading not required.)

Place	Date	Hour	Summary of Events and Information	Remarks and references to Appendices
2" Vlamertinghe	9th Jan		Battery to replace unserviceable	
"	28		Despatched to Base 14 Rifles from Motor Car driver. Returned another Travelling kitchen with Lantern and. 9" Rifle Brigade received & inspected Maxim gun from trenches. Reported this to Ordnance 2nd Army & demanded spare part for it. In response to enquiries from Ordnance 2nd Army replied that I estimated own to eight hundred Helmets a week would require repair.	
	29		Vickers Machine Gun received to day to replace an unserviceable one in charge of L. Motor Machine Gun Battery. Sent this gun. Went this afternoon to 9" Rifle Brigade repaired their gun. Went the afternoon to 9" Rifle Brigade to replace an unserviceable one. Returned to Base 10 Chiefs Foot & five Lewis stocks which from Princess Pattn.	

Army Form C. 2118.

WAR DIARY
or
INTELLIGENCE SUMMARY.
(Erase heading not required.)

Instructions regarding War Diaries and Intelligence Summaries are contained in F. S. Regs., Part II. and the Staff Manual respectively. Title pages will be prepared in manuscript.

Place	Date	Hour	Summary of Events and Information	Remarks and references to Appendices
S. Wamertigh.	1917 Jun 30		Water Cart for S'Khoshin L.I. arrived at Railhead from Base. Put in order that unserviceable telephones should be returned to me at once for repair by Signal Coy.	

Lieuten[ant] Col[onel]
Commdg 131st (Light) Division

1577 Wt. W10791/1773 500,000 1/15 D. D. & L. A.D.S.S./Forms/C. 2118.

14th Division

A.&.Q.S. 14th Division
Vol. II

1-31-4-15

Army Form C. 2118.

WAR DIARY
INTELLIGENCE SUMMARY.
(Erase heading not required.)

Instructions regarding War Diaries and Intelligence Summaries are contained in F.S. Regs., Part II. and the Staff Manual respectively. Title pages will be prepared in manuscript.

Hour, Date, Place	Summary of Events and Information	Remarks and references to Appendices

Confidential.

War Diary of :-
D.A.D.O.S. 14th Division.
(Major A. Williams Freeman)
A.O.D.

From : 1 . 7 . 15.
To : 31 . 7 . 15.

WAR DIARY
or
INTELLIGENCE SUMMARY
(Erase heading not required.)

Army Form C. 2118.

Place	Date	Hour	Summary of Events and Information	Remarks and references to Appendices
Wormhoudt	1915 July 2		Issued red screens to Infantry for indicating their position to Artillery. Sick I now in the Platoon.	
	3		Ten Vickers Guns arrived. Distributed me to each Battalion of 41st Infy Bde in fact completion of their establishment. The Brigade two runs 3 guns per Battalion. Reported above to D.A.D.S. 2nd Army Headqrs gun teams in were were trained by 9th Bigd. Bde. to 28 Division.	
	4		Indented for Bale to 20 Colt Mg3d attachments to Vickers Guns then officer equipment to obtain as frequent demands can not run complied with.	
	5		Indented in Bale to two Vickers Guns. Authority O.E. 456 Reported myself to D.D.V.S. 2nd Army in accordance with his instructions & explained the position of distribution of Machine Guns in Division.	

Army Form C. 2118.

WAR DIARY
or
INTELLIGENCE SUMMARY.

(Erase heading not required.)

Instructions regarding War Diaries and Intelligence Summaries are contained in F. S. Regs., Part II. and the Staff Manual respectively. Title pages will be prepared in manuscript.

Place	Date	Hour	Summary of Events and Information	Remarks and references to Appendices
2 Wormwood	1913 July 7		Instructions received that cloth & holdits for carrying the first Smoke Helmets is to be issued. To be worn on behind the left front of the S.D. Jacket. Pointed out in Bar accordingly. Instructions received that Helmets which have been subjected to Gas S.B.W. need not be withdrawn & rectified.	
	8		Issued Smoke Protectors to 4 & 2" Infy Bde.	
	9		2 Visitors M.O. arrived & viewed us to 9 C High Bde & am to 5 Cav & Bucks L.I. Put in evidence of Golum that the woolzo in most Helmets may great & that Co should endeavour by any means to rectify this.	
	10		Sew curtains for P's Cpls beginning to arrive. New Petalhiffs & new diffuse with the Telescopic Sights arrived. Issued Pethiffs 25 & 2 Bde to 4 & 2" Bde, 1 Bde to each of 41 & 43 Bde.	

1577 Wt. W10791/1773 500,000 1/15 D. D. & L. A.D.S.S./Forms/C. 2118.

Army Form C. 2118.

WAR DIARY
or
INTELLIGENCE SUMMARY.
(Erase heading not required.)

Place	Date 1916 July	Hour	Summary of Events and Information	Remarks and references to Appendices
2 Hamerton	10		Instructed to demand Reinmd Shrapnel to complete to 50 p.c. for the division	
	12		Asked Base if Mags Allg. Fuze T+P No 85 available & reported issue of 72. Issued 666 pairs of Bora Boyler for protection against jam shells to 42 & 64 M.B in French	
	13		Heard from Base that 40 Fuze Keys for Fuze No 85 Going Vent indented on Base for October to carry in 2" Smith Helmet. Certain Gun stores allowed to A.O.B 1030-108 Vrtd are not issued in England are now beginning to arm in shell proportion.	
	14		Three portable Light mountings for Vickers Guns arrived & issued to L.I. Inf.y Bde.	
	15		3 S.S Reinmd Shraphe arrived from Base & issued. Purchased 25 lb worth of Green Canvas for concealment of trenches &c.	

1577 Wt. W10791/1773 500,000 1/15 D. D. & L. A.D.S.S./Forms/C. 2118.

Army Form C. 2118.

WAR DIARY
or
INTELLIGENCE SUMMARY.
(Erase heading not required.)

Place	Date	Hour	Summary of Events and Information	Remarks and references to Appendices
L'Hamerlijk	1915 July 15		All incidents prior to June 1st cancelled at Base	
	16		Notification received that tunic is to be Based in Calais. Am in doubt to read Havre midnight 18th. Boys in US toys arrived today & distributed. Cannot put Cycle Mngs attachment to future Car & units are complaining	
	17		Sent in weekly return in requirements of Cars, Machine Guns, Clothing & Equipment. Drew special attention to the urgent need of S.A.A. testing tool & light Crain to A.S. Hosp (3 in); also to difficulty in obtaining Cylo Mngs attachment for Vickers Gun; also to the shortage of pantaloons arising from the Bott. Informed that detached is to be Bavenchove from 19th inst.	
	18.		Railhead altered to Caestre from 19"	

Army Form C. 2118.

WAR DIARY
or
INTELLIGENCE SUMMARY.
(Erase heading not required.)

Instructions regarding War Diaries and Intelligence Summaries are contained in F. S. Regs., Part II. and the Staff Manual respectively. Title pages will be prepared in manuscript.

Place	Date	Hour	Summary of Events and Information	Remarks and references to Appendices
2 Mountigh	1915 July 19.		Informed D.D.O.S. 2nd Army alteration of Railhead 11 Liverpots Ltd Vickers Gun Badly damaged. Forwarded first one & informed D.D.O.S. 2nd Army.	
"	21.		Visited 7th K.R.R. & 7th Bde. Instructed to demand fire Vickers gun. Distribution to be seen to each 7 & 8 K.R.R. 7 & 8 Bde. 9 R. Bde. Division Gun under with Corps from today.	
"	22		5th Ox & Bucks. L.I. 2nd Vickers Gun damaged by enemy's fire. Forwarded to replace.	
"	23		Division comes under Sixth Corps from noon today. 6750 Inst. Helmets arrived from Base. Despatched 122 Rifles belonging to R.A.	
"	24		4000 Inst. Helmets arrived 6/10 Vickers gun for 5 Ox & Bucks. L.I. Forwarded weekly report on Priority requirements.	

Army Form C. 2118.

WAR DIARY
or
~~INTELLIGENCE SUMMARY.~~
(Erase heading not required.)

Place	Date	Hour	Summary of Events and Information	Remarks and references to Appendices
R. Vlamertinghe	1915 July 26		Two Machine Guns arrived & distributed as soon as 21/25. This completes the L.T. Infantry Brigade to two per Battalion. Sent a local Indent to Ordnance to Boulogne, including about 200 18 Pdr. Cartridge Cases. Returned to C.R.A my inability to get the return of an unexercised did right from one of the Batteries. Received 5223 rounds 18lb rounds from Bdes. This amplifies my demand for Reserve, but owing to losses & provision for 60fts it will I think be necessary to put forward a supplementary demand.	
"	27		Stores coming up well from Calais & many buoy outstanding indents being cleared off.	
"	28		Load of Salvage dispatched.	
"	30		Division Landshut returns severely to day & seven trenches lost but no exact details available at present. 14 Salfly Column + 14 "	

WAR DIARY
INTELLIGENCE SUMMARY

Army Form C. 2118.

Place	Date	Hour	Summary of Events and Information	Remarks and references to Appendices
2nd Wanneville	1915 July 30		Ammunition Sub-Park came under me for supplies.	
	31.		Losses in yesterday's equipment severe. I also learn that some machine guns in charge of A.S.C. 13d. Sgd. Tan have lost their units unable to furnish me with details at present. This appears also to be some losses in equipment & clothing, but in a supplementary indent the in anticipation of extra demands.	

A. Williams - Freeman Major
A.D.S.S./16. Sier
1.8.15

14th Division

121/6607

Headquarters 14th Division
S.A.D.O.S.

Vol: III

From 1 - 31. 5. 15

Confidential.

War Diary
of
Major Williams-Freeman, D.A.D.O.S. 14' Division.

from Aug 1st/15 to August 31st/15.

Place	Date	Hour	Summary of Events and Information	Remarks and references to Appendices
R. Vlamertinghe	1915 Aug. 1st		There was a heavy bombardment during the night by our guns. At about 1pm received information that our guns of L/B Bryced were out of action owing to failure of running out springs. Sent Capt. J.O.M. Stitch him to obtain guns & was informed that he had put them right. Demanded in Base for two outer running out springs for 18 pr. A.C. who had used this for use of the Batteries. 6 R.B.Y. L.L. Zed Limbered C.S. were destroyed by shell fire. Demanded to replace. Tea that infantry Corn had a considerable amount of gear including gun machine guns. Demanded in Base for 4 Vickers guns to replace casualties (1 2 R.B. Horn, of R.B. m) also gun clothing & accessories in anticipation of heavy demands on us. AWL	
"	2		Indented in Base for 50 inner spring case. Saw J.O.M. who informed me that the main cause of the trouble with L.P. Bell was lack of oil in the Buffers. This was caused the faulty plates	

WAR DIARY
or
INTELLIGENCE SUMMARY

Army Form C. 2118

Place	Date	Hour	Summary of Events and Information	Remarks and references to Appendices
1. Hazebrouck	1915 Aug 2.		He had repaired 2 guns by 6 p.m. Another in Park to be brought in. Indented in Base for an Vickers Gun for 1st K.R.R. to replace one damaged by shell fire, also for 6000 field dressings in anticipation of large demands. Things fairly quiet to day.	AWR
	3.		Received instructions from Ordnance 2nd Army to demand Vickers guns from Havre in front completion of est. Bt. 2 month. Complied. Received from Calais five Vickers guns in Brighton to my demand for six, in 1st + 2nd 6/10 fm from 49 Division. Completed all Casualties + ran remainder in cart to 6 D.C.L.I. S. Yorkshires + 9th K.R.R.C. Received report from I.O.M. that an 10 Polrejun in charge of B/4b was unserviceable. Demanded in Havre to replace. Other things fairly quiet to day. Sent P.Cox to Rail Station.	AWR
	4.		Poperinghe was shelled during the night + my staff thought it prudent to evacuate the Store. They are working well though rather a strenuous time.	AWR

Army Form C. 2118

WAR DIARY
or
INTELLIGENCE SUMMARY.
(Erase heading not required.)

Instructions regarding War Diaries and Intelligence Summaries are contained in F. S. Regs., Part II. and the Staff Manual respectively. Title pages will be prepared in manuscript.

Place	Date	Hour	Summary of Events and Information	Remarks and references to Appendices
Littlemord inthe	1915 Aug. 4		A large quantity of salvage was brought down to day some of which I issued to units & some returned to base. AWB	
"	5		A lot more salvage came in & I sent away two loads to Railhead. Went to see D.O.S. 2nd Army on subject of allotment of Machine Guns which was becoming rather complex. All now clear. Battering shelled again to day. AWB	
"	6		Heard from Havre that 6 Vickers Guns despatched. Informed D.O.S. Sent away more salvage. Received information about 6.30 pm from C.R.A. that an 4.5 Howitzer "smashed to pieces" by direct hit. He requested me to wire for another complete with carriage & all complements. Complied and informed D.D.O.S. 2nd Army & Brig. Commdr. Horse show to day. AWB	
"	7		Inspected damaged 4.5 Howitzer & came to the conclusion that it was beyond local repair. Carriage was badly strained & twisted & all	

1577 Wt. W10791/1773 500,000 1/15 D. D. & L. A.D.S.S./Forms/C. 2118.

WAR DIARY or INTELLIGENCE SUMMARY

Army Form C. 2118

Place	Date	Hour	Summary of Events and Information	Remarks and references to Appendices
Vlamertinghe	1915 Aug. 7		Fittings on left S. gun smashed. Ordered it to be taken to 6' Corps workshops for examination. Considerable quantity of lewis guns arrived which will fit up the division. Heard that 18 Pdr. & 4·5 Hob. to 46 Col left on 6 AWB	
	8		Heard from Havre that 4·5 Howitzer Ind. left. 18 Pdr. arrived & taken to 8' Corps Shops. Saw J.O.M. 5' Corps. Visited Railhead. Three Travelling kitchens arrived for 13' Infantry, 5' Yorkshires, 9' K.R.R. Instr. that the scale has been strengthened. This 9' bn. will draw & sansers. Wired to Vickers Guns to replace us lost by 11' Sherwoods. I hear that 10' Sherwoods & 7' K.R.R. Jam said an unserviceable un. AWB	
	9		Big Bombardment by our guns during night accompanied. I understand the desired success. 83 Battery 49' Bde. It reported field light & carrier damaged. Can three & spare carrier but lack no spare light. Unobtained C.R.A. borrowed un. from L.6 Div.	

WAR DIARY
or
INTELLIGENCE SUMMARY

Army Form C. 2118

Place	Date	Hour	Summary of Events and Information	Remarks and references to Appendices
R'Vlamertinghe	1915 Aug 9.		Information received from I.O.M. that carriage & cradle of 18 Pdr. gun which was damaged on 3rd instant (see report under that date) are also unserviceable. Demanded accordingly from Havre. The gun arrived yesterday & this will cause some delay in mounting it. Instructions received from 6' Corps to draw tents for 1000 men from O.D. 2nd Corps Troops & hand over 2.1 f to 49th Division. Arranged to do this tomorrow. Took over 199 shelters from O.D. 6' Corps. Consulted O.T.O. 3rd Division in future in 6' periscopes for R.A.	
"		10	Sent damaged Hill Sight to 2nd Corps for repair & carrier to 5' Corps. Received information that 2 Fisher guns destroyed or damaged by enemy's fire. All belong to 2 & 3rd British but impossible to discover at present to what units. Accordingly demanded three guns & two torpedos from 6' Summits. Can distribute Peter. Instructions also received to demand eight	

WAR DIARY
or
INTELLIGENCE SUMMARY

Army Form C. 2118

(Erase heading not required.)

Place	Date	Hour	Summary of Events and Information	Remarks and references to Appendices
R: Manneville	1915 Aug 10"		Vickers guns from Havre & in receipt to hand me from to 49" Division to replace those received on loan from them. This will complete the Division up to establishment. Vickers guns demanded for 11" Lunsford in 8" Instant arrived & was issued. R.W.F.	
"		11ᵃᵐ	The three Vickers Guns demanded yesterday arrived this morning from Calais. Brisk work! Received instruction from 43" Bde M.G. Officer that the three two reported as lost are damaged. He will inform me unit as soon as furnish. 19.44.5 Smoke Helmets arrived. This is to complete issue of 2 per man. G.O. & A.M.C. instructed me not to issue until arrival of satchels. Hastened those from Scott. W.T.	‖
"	12"		I find that the three Maxim Guns which arrived yesterday on Manouvre in lieu of Vickers not at present available. The Vickers will	

WAR DIARY

or INTELLIGENCE SUMMARY

Army Form C. 2118

Place	Date	Hour	Summary of Events and Information	Remarks and references to Appendices
Wormhoudt	1915 Aug 12		So went up as soon as available when the Maxims & spare parts are to be returned. Under the circumstances I was instructed not to issue to the present. The three damaged guns have been returned to me, two badly damaged & one slightly. I am ordered to have them depleted to spare tomorrow. They belonged one to 6.D.C.L.I. & two to 6.K.O.Y.L.I. Visited 6 Corps Workshops in the afternoon & arranged about repair of Water Carts. AWT	11
	13		I received instructions this morning to issue the 3 Maxims to Brigade Machine Gun Officer of 43rd Bde, who would I possibly told them intact as reserve. Visited D.D.O.S. 2nd Army in afternoon & explained the position, also that as regards small Helmets Vis. 5" Cir & Bucket reported they had a behind gun knocked out I autom. & that all spare parts had been lost or destroyed. Inspected two guns & ammunition to replace. AWT	

WAR DIARY
INTELLIGENCE SUMMARY

Army Form C. 2118

Place	Date	Hour	Summary of Events and Information	Remarks and references to Appendices
A. Vlamertinghe	1915 Aug 15th		Zinc Tubes arrived to day & distributed as follows:— 2 to 5th Ox & Bucks, 2 to 11th Lanfusil, & on chart to 10th Durhams. The remaining two I landed on to 49th Divn. in repayment of loan from them. The Divisn is now supplied with Zinc Tubes for Battns. except that two tubes are required in exchange for two brass Sprinkle was chilled last night but they avoided my store. Inspected from the Nolat Senst Helmets to Car Enfant 2nd Army for testing.	AWL
	16		Rode to I.C.L.I. Servcort Transport Lines. They have been using their half socks for taking return to the trenches & find they require some more. Loose hair for stuffing the flannell. Demanded 56lb. Received instructions to demand Two Pattern Smoke Helmets for R.A., R.E. & Infantry. Demanded 1635D. These are for use as Second Helmet.	AWL

WAR DIARY
or
INTELLIGENCE SUMMARY
(Erase heading not required.)

Army Form C. 2118

Place	Date	Hour	Summary of Events and Information	Remarks and references to Appendices
2. Ylamertinghe	1915 Aug. 17		Received instructions from D.D.S. 2nd Army that Tub Pattern Helmet are for the present only to be issued to Officers & N.C.O's with R.A. Inf. & Fd. Coys. Accordingly amended my demand in this Bde. Visited 6th Cdn Wks. Coy. Found a great pressure of work there & in consequence my repairs to Webe Carts Kitchens &tc. not getting on very fast. RWJ.	—
	18.		The Kitchen frames arrived to replace the two Maurms which were issued from the Base a short while ago. Visited Town Major Poperinghe with a view to finding a suitable place for Armourers Shop. Two Labour M.Ps visited Head Quarters today with complaints to them the shortage in sum stores &c. RWJ.	
	20		In conjunction with O.C. Pioneer Battn. selected site for Armourers Shop. Horse shoes arrived except certain sizes. Hastened them from Base. RWJ.	

Army Form C. 2118

WAR DIARY
or
INTELLIGENCE SUMMARY
(Erase heading not required.)

Place	Date	Hour	Summary of Events and Information	Remarks and references to Appendices
Vlamertinghe	1915 Aug 22		Received 1750 Tub Pattern Helmets from 3rd Division also 500 each from 17 & 50 Divisions. Issued according to programme received from 6 Corps. Visited Hut Lofts. Cummins arrived from Ypres & started shift about my store. A.W.T	
"	23	1680	Tub Helmets arrived from Base. Arranged issue with Corps Staff. C.O. visited store & Cummins shift & discussed the question of how many Cummins were required here. A.W.T	
"	25	1690	Tub Helmets arrived from Base. Arranged distribution. Sent to Armentieres & ordered 500 blouses to carrying bombs. Inspected Farm that I thought might be suitable for store. A.W.T	
"	26	2310	Tub Helmets arrived from Base. Arranged distribution. Visited Fifth Corps Workshops & Railhead. Put forward application that Farm mentioned above might be allotted to me for store. A.W.T	

Army Form C. 2118

WAR DIARY

(Erase heading not required.)

Place	Date	Hour	Summary of Events and Information	Remarks and references to Appendices
Wamertinghe	1915 Aug 26/27		A.A. & Q.M.G. does not approve of my changing position of my store at present. I am to bring forward the question again if shelling gets worse. Visited S.O.S. 2nd Army & explained position of smoke helmets & discussed other question. Called at Fifth Corps HQrs. 140 Tube Helmets arrived, also 1000 Satchels. AWR	
"	28		4460 Tube Helmets arrived, also 2000 Satchels. AWR	
"	29		8330 Tube Helmets arrived. This completes to under man & officer. Reported S.S.O.S. that I had approximately 16000 respirators to dispose, also that Batteries had received 24 cycles each. AWR	
"	30		7000 Satchels arrived. Arranged issue.	
"	31		Received instructions from S.S.O.S. 2nd Army to hand over 2330 Tube Helmets to 46' Div. & to return 1600 Respirators to Calais. AWR	

121/6930.

11th Division

H.Q. 14th Division
S.A.S.O.
Vol: IX
Sep 1. 15

Enclosure to 121/6607

      The attached War diary is sent to you for
your information. Please pass it, when you have done
with it, to M.O.1. for inclusion in 121/6607

      Should you desire to take any action in
regard to subjects dealt with in the Diary, please
extract from it what is required and send such extract up
for registration stating on this paper that you have done
so.

                      A. C. PEDLEY.

                      17/9/15.

A.u.G.

If you have time to read this is rather a good typical diary of a Divisional Ordnance Officer. Touches on various points, Salvage, replacements, repairs &c..

Quite good & satisfactory

18/9

Confidential.

War Diary
of
Major A. Williams-Freeman
D.A.D.O.S.
14 Division

From 1st Sept. 1915 to 30 Sept. 1915.

Army Form C. 2118

WAR DIARY

or

~~INTELLIGENCE SUMMARY~~

(Erase heading not required.)

Instructions regarding War Diaries and Intelligence Summaries are contained in F. S. Regs., Part II. and the Staff Manual respectively. Title pages will be prepared in manuscript.

Place	Date	Hour	Summary of Events and Information	Remarks and references to Appendices
Vlamertinghe	1915 Sept. 2		Received instructions from D.D.S. 2nd Army that all Respirators with Troops to be withdrawn within this condition & retained by me pending further instructions. Sun case water Totly arrived. Visited C Battery 49 Bde. This had last Zed been allowed to put into Zed condition. Visited the Sixth Corps Workshops. AWT	
"	3		Ordered two kitchens in charge of S. Staffordshire L.I. to be taken to Workshops for repair. Both with broken axles. AWT	
"	4		9000 Blankets arrived. By them I was ordered to hand over 4,500 to 17 Divn. Called on D.D.S. 2nd Army. Instructed to Visit Jun 6 to replace an unserviceable one of the I.C.L.I. AWT	
"	5		300 Blankets arrived c/60 Vichie Jun but as the I.C.L.I. Jun was found serviceable I returned it to Base & informed D.D.S. Sent to Cementieres re Sum purchases. AWT	

Army Form C. 2118

WAR DIARY

or

~~INTELLIGENCE SUMMARY~~

(Erase heading not required.)

Instructions regarding War Diaries and Intelligence Summaries are contained in F. S. Regs., Part II. and the Staff Manual respectively. Title pages will be prepared in manuscript.

Place	Date	Hour	Summary of Events and Information	Remarks and references to Appendices
J. Hamartyh 6.	1915 Sept.			
	14		Proceeded on leave. AWR	
	15		Returned from leave. Went through cowspheres which had come in during my absence. Found everything normal. AWR	
	17.		D.C.A.M.C. and D.S.O.S 2nd Army inspected my store and divisional Ammunition Dept. AWR	
	18.		10 tents and 6 Sayers stores arrived. Also 16 Ammunition wagons & limbers for L.9. sent in place of G.S. wagons. I listened charge number of items due on indents. Also forwarded a return of Priority requirements. AWR	
	19		10 tents arrived making 6 total of 20 received. AWR	
	20.		Brigade Machine Gun Officers of 42nd & 43rd Brigades reported	

1577 W. W10791/1773 500,000 1/15 D. D. & L. A.D.S.5.(Forms)/C. 2118.

Army Form C. 2118

WAR DIARY
or
~~INTELLIGENCE SUMMARY~~

(Erase heading not required.)

Instructions regarding War Diaries and Intelligence Summaries are contained in F. S. Regs., Part II. and the Staff Manual respectively. Title pages will be prepared in manuscript.

Place	Date	Hour	Summary of Events and Information	Remarks and references to Appendices
Rt Flammertz	1917 Sept 20		Several deficiencies of Machine Gun parts. Wired to Base to complete. AWZ	
	21		Proceeded to Dunkirk for local purchases. 550 Lt.Wm Buckle arrived. B.M.G.O. 43" Bde. reported a Machine Gun of K.O.Y.L.I. damaged. Indented to replace, although it is possible the armourers may be able to repair it. AWB	
	22.		Machine Gun to K.O.Y.L.I. arrived & issued. Despatched damaged gun to Base. Went to St Omer to make local purchases. AWZ	
	23.		An eighteen pounder of A/Hy scelly bulged. T.O.M. reports gun and carriage unserviceable. Indented to replace rejecting wire to 2nd Army and communications. Same M.G. ports for 42 & 43" Bdes arrived and issued. 20 standard boxes filled known comm. AWZ	

WAR DIARY
INTELLIGENCE SUMMARY

Army Form C. 2118

Place	Date	Hour	Summary of Events and Information	Remarks and references to Appendices
K'Navantigh	1915 Aug. 24.		Received report from Brigade Machine Gun Officer that 2 Vickers Gun and Tripod Left Gun destroyed. Indented on Base to replace. A Gun carriage I 03/48 was rendered unserviceable. to Christ Lit. J.D.M. succeeded in making one serviceable Gun and carriage from the serviceable parts of 2 Gun I 03/48. AW	
"	25		Several guns out of action after heavy bombardment early this morning. Main trouble appears to be buffers. Return out springs do not appear to be very satisfactory as their life is comparatively short. Great demand for them. 6 Vickers Gun I 10 to Ourhanie reported damaged. Wired to Base to replace. AW	
"	26.		Visited 6" Corps H.Qrs. There there seems to be rather a shortage then of buffer parts e.g. strips, spring, parting plates etc. 6 Gun I C/49 L27 just came in with a direct hit in the trail. Gun itself appears to be all right except the breech mechanism. AW	

WAR DIARY
or
INTELLIGENCE SUMMARY
(Erase heading not required.)

Army Form C. 2118

Place	Date	Hour	Summary of Events and Information	Remarks and references to Appendices
Willamertinghe	1915 Sept 26		Two Vickers Guns & spare parts arrived for 6' K.O.Y.L.I. (to replace one destroyed) and for 10' Durham (to replace damaged). Four Vickers guns of 4.2" Bde. (2 9" R Bde & 2 10' Durham) reported lost in action with "Hotchkiss" mont of spare parts demanded in above accordingly. Henry Aust. Gun Ammunition wgn for 13/49 arrived. 1551 pair of Gum boots arrived. A.W.T	
"	27.		18 Pdr. Gun and carriage arrived for A/47. Instructed them to fetch it & return Buffel one to Railhead for transmission to Base. Indented on Base for a 18 Pdr. carriage to replace one of C/47 damaged by direct hit. A.W.T	
"	28		A/47 took the Buffel Gun to Railhead. Reported this to C.H.A. and D.D.O.S. 2nd Army. Handed over 3500 Ordinary Smoke Helmets to 2nd Canadian Division. This finished my surplus. Indented for Water Cart for 6'D.C.L.I. to replace one fractured by I.D.M. Guns indented for on 26" MSC Guns arrived. A.W.T	

Army Form C. 2118.

WAR DIARY
or
INTELLIGENCE SUMMARY
(Erase heading not required.)

Place	Date	Hour	Summary of Events and Information	Remarks and references to Appendices
R/Hemertinge	1915 Sept 29.		A further consignment of 1509 Gun Boots arrived. Also 448 Lambs Hurricane Lamps in tins. Indented for rear portion Limbered Wagon for 10" Turbans to replace one damaged. Cannot yet any definite information from 42nd Bde. as to their Machine Gun losses in recent action. A.W.F.	
"	30		Issued completed 9" R.B. & 6" G. v Buds with 2 Vickers Guns each & share parts. Find that 9" R.B. an definite & another Gun & other units in the Brigade of certain Gun parts and components. Indented to replace. Received report from I.O.M. that a Gun of C/46 bat/ted and unserviceable, also carriers unserviceable. Instructed Battery to remove Gun and carriage to Railhead. Indent as now coming in from 4.2" Bde. to replace a considerable amount of equipment lost on 25". Sent L.O.O. of 9" Division which is coming up the line from 1st Army. AWF	A.Williams Lieutenant SAF 27 M.G.O.

121/7433

14th Hussain

AQ. 14th Hu: SASOS.
vol: 5

Oct 15

Conf̱

War Diary
of
D.A.D.O.S.
14th Division.

1-10-15
 to
31-10-15

Confidential.

War Diary

of

Major A. P. Williams Freeman
D.A.D.O.S. 14 Division

from 1st Oct. 1915 to 31st Oct. 1915

WAR DIARY
or
INTELLIGENCE SUMMARY

(Erase heading not required.)

Army Form C. 2118

Place	Date	Hour	Summary of Events and Information	Remarks and references to Appendices
R/Hamerting	1915 Oct. 1		Vickers Gun demanded for 9" Rifle Brigade to replace one not arrived. Asked D.A.D.S. 2nd Army if Tent Bottoms were available now available but that provision had been made. AWB	
	2		18 Pdr. Gun & Carriage arrived at Railhead for 46 Bde to replace one unserviceable through defect. Reported to Ordnance G.H.Q. & 2nd Army that only of Gun would be taken to Renticed on 3rd Wgn limbered G.S. arrived for 10' Durham L.I. to replace one unserviceable. Indented for Tripod mounting for 10' Durham L.I. Visited D' Corps whs 2 Sp. AWB	
	3		Went carefully through returns indents of 41" Inf. Bde & 46 Bde R.F.A. informed that 43" Inf. Bde were to be attached temporarily to 5' Corps but to be administered by us. AWB	

WAR DIARY
~~INTELLIGENCE SUMMARY~~

Army Form C. 2118

Place	Date	Hour	Summary of Events and Information	Remarks and references to Appendices
R. Nieuwertingh	1917 Oct 4		Divisional Bomb school to be formed. Consulted with C.S.O. 2 as to what to fit them out with in the way of Tents cooking utensils &c. Visited 6 Corps stores. Poperinghe Shelled heavily about 10am. RWT	
"	6		A further 260 Tents arrived from Base. Forwarded demand for 260 Lamps Hurricane accordingly. I am sent to Base nearly 1000 rifles in the last few days. They come in in a very bad state but all can been cleaned & oiled. RWT	
"	7		D.D.O.S. 2nd Army visited my store. He gave me permission to purchase £100 worth of Hurricane Lamps. Sent off Under Holland at one & spent last four in Vickers gun arrived. Handed over two to 2nd Division & reported accordingly to Haute Clair. Pointed out to D.D.O.S. the enormous consumption of Rifle Head. He suggested demanding more Chain collar. RWT	

WAR DIARY
INTELLIGENCE SUMMARY

(Erase heading not required.)

Army Form C. 2118

Place	Date	Hour	Summary of Events and Information	Remarks and references to Appendices
	1915 Oct			
2 Vlamertinghe	8		No Horse Shoe size 8 Hind came up. Last week also demand was cut down. Reported this by wire to D.D.S. 2nd Army. AWT	
"	9		A further 100 tents arrived from Boe without any staining material. Demanded another 100 tents Hurricane. A further consignment of Rum Jars also arrived making total received 3500. Completed puncheons of Hurricane Lamps to the value of just short of £100. AWT	
"	10		17 Bicycles arrived. This nearly completes my draws out. 3420 pairs of woollen drawers also arrived. This is the first consignment of warm clothing. Two of my staff now on leave rather short handed at the Dump. So told Cmdr. Holland to spend most of his time then on the front. AWT	

WAR DIARY
or
INTELLIGENCE SUMMARY.
(Erase heading not required.)

Army Form C. 2118.

Place	Date	Hour	Summary of Events and Information	Remarks and references to Appendices
K: Vlamertinghe	1915 Oct. 12		3 Telescopic Sighted Rifles arrived and issue made one to each Infantry Bde. 42nd Infy. Bde. report that they are short of Pistol Very & Pistol Illuminating 1½" owing to losses in action on 25th only one indent is in for Pistol Very & that dated 10th June for Pistols 1½". Suggested they go into the trenches tomorrow. Sanction to to discover their deficiencies.	
"	13		Some Peaches for Limbered G.S. wagons arrived. They have been sent into training.	
"	14		Reference Serial of Winter Clothing, asked I.S.O.S. if Colo Winter be demanded 6 to replace U/S only. He confirmed. Auth demanded Wilkinson for Y.K.R.R. to replace one damaged by shell fire and.	
"	15		Special Scale of Winter clothing issued. I.S.O.S. asked for explanation of reason for demanding Claim Collar for Horses. Forwarded by I.R.L.S.	

WAR DIARY
or
INTELLIGENCE SUMMARY
(Erase heading not required.)

Army Form C. 2118

Instructions regarding War Diaries and Intelligence Summaries are contained in F.S. Regs., Part II. and the Staff Manual respectively. Title pages will be prepared in manuscript.

Place	Date	Hour	Summary of Events and Information	Remarks and references to Appendices
R.Mamatrik	1917 Oct 15		Unservicable Sun & L.K.R.R. returned to Bas. A further 300 Tubs washing arrived. G.O.S. Limbrick wired fr. 48 Sdn. A.C. arrived to complete establishment. Obtained authority to purchase 2 L.D. Ben & Canus fr 2000 Francs Aust.	
"	16		Vickers Gun for L'K.R.R. arrived. Forwarded demand for 3 G.S. wagons - complete. Turned fr. I.A.C. on increase of establishment according to Patent G.F.G.1098. Aust.	
"	17		Sergeant Wood G.D. from Clair reported his arrival for a course of instruction as Brigad Warrant Officer. Attached him to Sub-Condr. Wittle & gave him short lecture on the general system. Then of the kitchens in charge of S'omerset L.I. refused to lean boilers ankles. Aust.	
"	18		100 Latrine Buckets arrived from Bar. Also 225 pairs of Gum	

Place	Date	Hour	Summary of Events and Information	Remarks and references to Appendices
R. Wamertinghe	1915 Oct. 18		Both High. distributed letter as follows 6 to each Bde. Hd. Ars. R.F.A. 12 to each Battery & 21 to 42nd Infy. Bde. AWP	
	19.		Decided to change the Armourers in civil shot every 3 months, also that the Brigade in that area should scan the use of all the armourers still at Rest. No troops up to day. AWP	
"	20.		Arm. Sergts & 6 Smiths & L.C.L.I. returned to their units in accordance with above. Visited 6 Corps workshops. Informed that about 105 sets of tents bottoms will arrive at Railhead every other day from 22nd instant. AWP	
	22.		70 tent Bottoms arrived. Transport wanted. Forwarded indents for special winter clothing. Body bands (number many) arrived. AWP	
	23.		42nd Infy. Bde. are now in Rest area & a considerable distance back. ?	

WAR DIARY
or
INTELLIGENCE SUMMARY.
(Erase heading not required.)

Army Form C. 2118

Place	Date	Hour	Summary of Events and Information	Remarks and references to Appendices
Hamerlingh	1917 Oct 23		am Therefore sending on lorry daily to refilling point with stores for the Brigade. Good instructions for units as well as my own people. Went to Bailleul to try & purchase Braziers. Sent to G 2nd. Received suggestion from D.O.S. that winter clothing should be demanded in an additional bulk day & that it should arrive at Railhead on Tuesday's. Replied that I would prefer that the items be divided over the week & that Tuesday be still kept a "free day".	AnR.
	24		Owing to a misunderstanding, the lorry went to the wrong refilling point this morning. 53 sets tent bottoms received to day & issued.	AnR.
	25		200 Braziers received to day — part of the 400 allotted this Division. Received instructions to send Sergeant Wood to 51st Division.	AnR.
	26		3 Limbered R.E. wagons arrived to 89'Coy. to replace unserviceable.	AnR.

WAR DIARY
or
INTELLIGENCE SUMMARY

(Erase heading not required.)

Army Form C. 2118

Place	Date	Hour	Summary of Events and Information	Remarks and references to Appendices
2: Flamertyp	1915 Oct 27.		Sergeant Wood who has been attached for instruction left this morning to join 51st Division. Visited Camp D.6 Somerset. Obtained sanction for purchase of a further 400 Bomb Carriers at 2000 francs. Sent two lorries to Dunkerque for 50 Tellos. AWR.	
"	28		6000 Undercoats fur arrived as an advance instalment. Suggested issue of 500 to each Battalion. Find that reinforcements are arriving without blankets. This has rather upset my calculations & am short of them. Two of my lorries broken down today; 9" Division rifled me out with two. AWR.	
	29.		Base have not sent me any Sizes 9 Hind Horse shoes for the past three weeks. Reported this to SSO of 2nd Army. AWR.	
	30		A large quantity of clothing & 500 Horse rugs arrived today in addition to 466 trucks of Tent Bottoms. Rather difficult to	

WAR DIARY

Army Form C. 2118

Place	Date	Hour	Summary of Events and Information	Remarks and references to Appendices
Vlamertinghe	30 Oct 15/15		Complete with 1 cell. Began the issue of underwear to 1.1", 1.2" & 1.3" Infy. Bde in sets of 500 per Bn. Water cart arrived for 1st Durham L.I. Four kilt bands trousers arrived & were issued 2 to 41" Bde & 2 to six bomb throwers. Sent to Armentières for 40 French carriers. AWR	
"	31		2500 Gum Boots thigh arrived, also more tent bottoms. AWR	

A.Williams. Major.
Freeman. A.D.S. 1st Div.

HQ 14th Division
Vol: 6

121/7708

Bde.

Nov 15

Confidential.

War Diary
of
S.A.A.D.S. 14" (Light) Division
from Nov: 1st 1915 to Nov. 30 1915.

A Williams
Lieutenant Major
S.A.A.D.S. 14 Div.

Army Form C. 2118

WAR DIARY
or
INTELLIGENCE SUMMARY.
(Erase heading not required.)

Instructions regarding War Diaries and Intelligence Summaries are contained in F. S. Regs., Part II. and the Staff Manual respectively. Title pages will be prepared in manuscript.

Place	Date	Hour	Summary of Events and Information	Remarks and references to Appendices
1/Leicesters	1915 Nov 1		I reported to D.A.D.S. that amongst the consignment of Gum Boots Thigh received yesterday were a number of sizes 6 v 7. I said that I considered these sizes were too small & asked if they might be exchanged. Sent Lorry to Steenvoorde for furniture purchased. AWR	
	2		One C.S.M. & one Corporal C.S. Wigg arrived for 47 B.A.C. to complete establishment. I put forward the question as to who is responsible for the supply of raw material (iron steel &c) to Division Workshops. It is mainly used for the construction of Trench Stoves & should therefore I think, be supplied by R.E. AWR	
	3		A quantity of stoves wanted, stoves firebricks & & further consignment of coats undercoat for arrival today. AWR	
	4		The 2500 pairs of Gum Boots Thigh were today by orders of 6 Corps handed over to 6" & 49 Divisions. The order arrived just as I had 2/um	

1577 Wt.W10791/1773 500,000 1/15 D. D. & L. A.D.S.S./Forms/C. 2118.

Army Form C. 2118

WAR DIARY
or
~~INTELLIGENCE~~ SUMMARY
(Erase heading not required.)

Place	Date	Hour	Summary of Events and Information	Remarks and references to Appendices
K. Vlamertinghe	1915 Nov 3		Distribution of kit in another hour most of them would have gone. It is rather a mystery as to why they have been taken from us. AWZ	
	4		Another consignment of Tent Bottoms arrived today. I sent a W.O. to check them into the transport. AWZ	
	5		Horse shoes arrived. No shortage this week except that size 6" Hind sent in place of Size 9 Hind. Went to 6 Corps Workshops. AWZ	
	6		A further consignment of Tent Bottoms arrived & issued. Heard today that Divl. Hd. Qrs are to move shortly to the Chateau at Vlamertinghe. AWZ	
	7		1500 mountains of Gum Boots arrived. This completes the allotted for. AWZ	

Army Form C. 2118

WAR DIARY
or
~~INTELLIGENCE SUMMARY~~
(Erase heading not required)

Instructions regarding War Diaries and Intelligence Summaries are contained in F.S. Regs., Part II. and the Staff Manual respectively. Title pages will be prepared in manuscript.

Place	Date	Hour	Summary of Events and Information	Remarks and references to Appendices
H. Vlamurtinghe	1915 Nov 8		Instructed to hand over 500 of the Gum Boots Thigh received yesterday to 49th Division. Sent to Dunkerque for further 2 40 Pairs	AD2
	9		A further consignment of Leather Jerkins arrived to day also the first consignment of Capo Mackintosh. Roll now of 58 to complete the Infantry with Former & the 43" Bd. with Latter.	AD2
	10		Issue of above proceeded. I also received instructions to hand over 500 Pairs of Gum Boots Thigh to 6 Div. & not to 49. the Balance (1000) to be distributed evenly amongst units of 43" Infy Bd.	AD2
	11		Capt Mr Holland to Dunkerque with two Lorries to fetch the Items ordered on 8th	AD2
	12		A large quantity of winter clothing came up to day but no verbs. Infantry are now complete in Leather Jerkins & worsted Gloves	

WAR DIARY

Army Form C. 2118.

Place	Date	Hour	Summary of Events and Information	Remarks and references to Appendices
R:Hamertinghe	1917 Nov. 12		Also 41½" & 43rd are practically complete with Capes Mackintosh, & all indents for Cardigans are clear. AWR	
"	13		Collected 44 sets Tent Bottoms from 17th Division. Sent under Holland to Armentières to put Bomb Carriers. These are to be issued to the Div. Bomb School. Blond Turner (R.C. & Q.M.C.) left today to take up new appointment. AWR	
	14		Three No. 14 Periscopes arrived to-day for the Batteries. Sent under Holland to Armentières to purchase items for store. AWR	
	15		6 Sniperscopes with Periscopes for Battalion arrived from Base today. Issue of all available winter clothing practically completed. AWR	
	16		No truck arrived today. Completed & further consignment of winter clothing. 100 Steel Helmets & 1000 Gas Goggles arrived on 15th AWR	

Army Form C. 2118

WAR DIARY

(Erase heading not required.)

Instructions regarding War Diaries and Intelligence Summaries are contained in F. S. Regs., Part II. and the Staff Manual respectively. Title pages will be prepared in manuscript.

Place	Date	Hour	Summary of Events and Information	Remarks and references to Appendices
Hannescamp	17		Issue of Goggles 3000 to 41" + 41", 42 + 43" Bdes + 31 Stl Helm G to 41", 42 + 43" Bdes. Ordered Sent lorry to D'Orcen to fetch 50 Braziers purchased locally. AW2	
	18		Visited G Corps Workshops. S.D.O.S. came to my store in afternoon but I missed him. Poleringhe was bombed this morning & by 5 or 6 aeroplanes. AWR.	
	19		Received information that m Lewis from being consigned to this division from Havre. It will be given to G. R. Bde. on arrival. 1000 Goggles received from G Corps. AWR	
	20		A further 100 Steel Helmets received to day. & to be issued to each Battalion AWR	
	21.		A further 4000 Goggles received from G Corps. Can complete Infantry	

WAR DIARY

Army Form C. 2118

Place	Date	Hour	Summary of Events and Information	Remarks and references to Appendices
R. Hamurtiga	1915 Nov 21		with thus. AWR	
"	22		The first consignment of second Blankets for men arrived today. Crowded to complete 6.4'' Infy. Bde. 14 Ammunition sub park moved to 6'' Corps Trench. AWR	
"	23		A further supply of blankets arrived. Issues continued. Disc clearing of Light Tripod Mountings for Machine Guns are beginning to arrive. Instructions received to demand 2nd Tube Helmets per man; to replace the present Hypo one. AWR	
"	24		Lewis Machine Guns arrived & issued to 8'' R. Bde. AWR	
"	25		More Blankets & 50 Trench Helmets arrived. Issued Letter 15 to each Bde. & 5 to Machine Gun Battery. AWR	

Army Form C. 2118.

WAR DIARY
or
INTELLIGENCE SUMMARY
(Erase heading not required.)

Place	Date	Hour	Summary of Events and Information	Remarks and references to Appendices
Killanvertigh	1917 Nov. 26		A further supply of Blankets arrived also 2000 Tube Helmets. Certain sizes of Horse Shoes did not come up. Reported same to D.D.O.S. 2nd Army. A suggestion received today that another shirt be issued in place of the vest which there is difficulty in getting supplies of. Wired to D.D.G.S. that G.O.C. preferred to wait for the vests. Ansd.	
"	27		1000 Vests arrived. To be issued to 41st Inf. Bde. Ansd.	
	28		Demand for horse shoes not fully complied with. Drew 2212 pairs of Gum boots Thigh from 6 Corps. Ansd.	
	29		Proceeded on leave. Ansd.	

A. Wilhurn
S.A.D.S. 16 Div.

Turman
Major
S.A.D.S. 16 Div.

S.A.S.O. 14th Div:
Fol: 7

Dec. 1915

WAR DIARY
or
INTELLIGENCE SUMMARY
(Erase heading not required.)

Army Form C. 2118.

Place	Date	Hour	Summary of Events and Information	Remarks and references to Appendices
Hazebrouck	1915 Dec. 6		Returned from Lean having been recalled owing to probable move of the Division from 2nd Army. Arrived at Hd. Qrs. about 3 pm	
"	7		Received instructions that winter clothing issued under C.R.O. is to be withdrawn. Cannot yet get programme until Division comes out of Trenches. AWP	
"	8		Saw A.D.O.S. 2nd Army & asked that Division might have priority since I view I certain articles, also that workshops should give us priority in the matter of repair to vehicles. This is arranged. I am to be transferred to 25 Division and Capt. Beckwith A.A.D.O.S. of that Division is to take on from me. AWP	
"	9		Arranged for 10 G.S. wagons I.S.A.C. to go to shops for repair. Try to send Wheelers. Visited 14 Bde. AWP	

Army Form C. 2118.

WAR DIARY
or
INTELLIGENCE SUMMARY.
(Erase heading not required.)

Place	Date	Hour	Summary of Events and Information	Remarks and references to Appendices
L'Hallobourg	1915 Dec. 10		Visited 6" Corps Workshops. Repairs to vehicles of S.A.C. proceeding satisfactorily. AWF	
	11		Went to see D.D.D.S. 2nd Army. The Fur Felt Helmets per man are to be carried in Bulk when this in move. Previous packing Cases is a difficulty. Asked Base if they can provide 680. Am also asking units to discover what they can, they should have no difficulty in getting sufficient number if they do this. 6000 Vests arrived today. AWF	
,,	12		Pickling gear arrived in good quantities today. Wired to Base for further supply of S.D. clothing to meet expected demands. Programme for packing in stores issued. AWF 200 sets Harness arrived	
,,	13		Col. Hole D.D.T. 2nd Army visited store this morning. 11,500 Vests arrived. This completes my demand. AWF	

WAR DIARY

~~INTELLIGENCE SUMMARY~~

(Erase heading not required.)

Army Form C. 2118.

Place	Date	Hour	Summary of Events and Information	Remarks and references to Appendices
B: Hazebrouck	15/3 14.		According to programme units began to return their winter clothing under special G.R.O. AuR	
"	15		A considerable amount of detail stores arrived also a large number of packing cases etc. & a quantity of forage shown though certain sizes still deficient. Captain Beckwith D.A.D.O.S. 25 Division arrived to take over from me. He is remaining in Reserve for the present & will superintend the store. AuR.	
"	16		Return of winter clothing proceeding. I am to report to 21st Division tomorrow to take over from Major Symonds. AuR.	
"	17.		Proceeded to Armentieres & reported to Hd Qrs 21st Division	AuR Freeman Major D.A.D.O.S. 14th Div C Williams D.A.D.O.S 14 Div

WAR DIARY
or
INTELLIGENCE SUMMARY
(Erase heading not required.)

Army Form C. 2118

Instructions regarding War Diaries and Intelligence Summaries are contained in F. S. Regs., Part II. and the Staff Manual respectively. Title Pages will be prepared in manuscript.

Place	Date	Hour	Summary of Events and Information	Remarks and references to Appendices
	1915			
Hazebrouck	17/12		Took over duties of D.A.D.O.S. 1st Division from Major Williams - Froms A.S.D.	MB
"	18/12		General routine & issue of stores at Poperinghe - taking in surplus stores and equipment in connection with impending move of division.	MB
"	19/12		ditto - Three enemy shells exploded in immediate vicinity of store - no casualties; slight damage to roof.	MB
"	20/12		Receiving surplus equipment & winter clothing from units. Issues of new stores to complete & general routine.	MB
"	21/12		Visited 2nd Army Workshops Baillieul to obtain repairs watches & telescopes; general routine store issues.	MB

WAR DIARY
or
INTELLIGENCE SUMMARY

(Erase heading not required.)

Army Form C. 2118

Instructions regarding War Diaries and Intelligence Summaries are contained in F. S. Regs., Part II. and the Staff Manual respectively. Title Pages will be prepared in manuscript.

Place	Date	Hour	Summary of Events and Information	Remarks and references to Appendices
Nieuwkerke	22/12		Urgent issues to Complete units' equipment to G.1038 scale before moving. Continued. Visited 6: Corps workshops and spoke officer regarding urgent repairs to vehicles.	MB
"	23/12		General routine work & urgent issues as on 22nd.	MB
"	24/12		General routine store & office work. Received instructions from H.Q. 14: Div: to "stand fast" regarding the move of division.	MB
"	25/12		Further instructions from 14: Divl. Hd.Q. that orders for move of division were cancelled. Units to be re-equipped with winter clothing and special stores which had been withdrawn & returned to Base.	MB
"	26/12		Winter clothing demands in bulk from Base; general routine.	MB
"	27/12		No special entries to record. Owing to move being cancelled, very small receipts only from Base.	MB

WAR DIARY
or
INTELLIGENCE SUMMARY

Army Form C. 2118

(Erase heading not required.)

Place	Date	Hour	Summary of Events and Information	Remarks and references to Appendices
Hazebrouck	1915 28/12		Normal routine services only.	MB
"	29/12		Receipt of winter clothing from Base, and distribution to units commenced.	MB
"	30/12		Prohibition of winter clothing continued. Proceeded to Armentières to arrange with civilian contractor for supply of grenade services urgently required to complete.	MB
"	31/12		Normal services only.	MB

N Berkworth Capt/RMG
D.A.D.S.S. 1st Army

BAOR. 14th Div.
Vol. 8

JAN 1916

Confidential

WAR DIARY
— of —
D.A.D.O.S. 14th DIVISION

1st January to 31st January 1916

N. Beckwith Capt.
D.A.D.O.S. 14th Div.

Army Form C. 2118

WAR DIARY
INTELLIGENCE SUMMARY
(Erase heading not required.)

Instructions regarding War Diaries and Intelligence Summaries are contained in F. S. Regs., Part II. and the Staff Manual respectively. Title Pages will be prepared in manuscript.

Place	Date	Hour	Summary of Events and Information	Remarks and references to Appendices
	1916			
Wormhoudt	1/1		General routine of store services. Visited D.A.D.O.S. 6th and 49th Divisional Ordnance Offices to obtain lists to urgently repaired for M.B. camps.	
"	2/1		Normal service only. Received 1500 pairs thigh gum boots for distribution.	M.B.
"	3/1		Visited late salvage dump 49th Div. Found large quantities of stores likely to be of further use. Arranged for working parts to sort over + collect servicable and unservicable articles. General routine work.	M.B.
"	4/1		General routine store issues. Salvaged over 900 rifles, 2000 bayonets, 28 wagon wheels, 23 limbers + other valuable stores from 49th Divnl. salvage dump.	M.B.
"	5/1		General routine Ordnance services.	M.B.

WAR DIARY
INTELLIGENCE SUMMARY

Army Form C. 2118

Place	Date	Hour	Summary of Events and Information	Remarks and references to Appendices
Plomonghil	1916 6/1		Annual Ordnance services - 750 steel helmets received and distributed	M.B.
"	7/1		Proceeded to Armentieres & collected female civilian contractor. No special events of service.	M.B.
"	8/1		Normal routine store & office duties	M.B.
"	9/1		ditto. Ditto. H.Q. 2nd Army Paid visit of inspection to store at Poperinghe. Called his attention to extensive wastage from H.Q.: Bomb dump.	M.B.
"	10/1		General mornings & store services. Proceeded to Esquelbecq in morning and obtained "Talbot" breakdown apparatus required for division.	M.B.
"	11/1		Visited 6: Corps workshops in connection with urgent repairs for new military supply section. General routine.	M.B.

WAR DIARY

INTELLIGENCE SUMMARY

(Erase heading not required.)

Army Form C. 2118

Instructions regarding War Diaries and Intelligence Summaries are contained in F.S. Regs., Part II. and the Staff Manual respectively. Title Pages will be prepared in manuscript.

Place	Date	Hour	Summary of Events and Information	Remarks and references to Appendices
	1916			
Hazebrouck	12/1		Normal issues of stores and Office routine. Collected 59 sacks of apts and 9 sacks from HQ; Distr. Salvage dump & returned same to Base.	MB
"	13/1		Proceeded to Bailleul to collect repaired telescopes & watches from 2nd Army workshops; left others for similar repairs. Normal routine.	MB
"	14/1		Proceeded to Armentières and arranged manufacture of rifle breech covers urgently required for duty; Bns. General routine.	MB
"	15/1		General routine store & Office duties. 100 trench helmets received from Base. Proceeded to Bailleul and otherwise repaired watches from 2nd Army workshops.	MB
"	16/1		General routine service. Proceeded on leave to England in evening.	MB
"	18/1		On leave MB	
"	19/1			

WAR DIARY
INTELLIGENCE SUMMARY
(Erase heading not required.)

Army Form C. 2118

Place	Date 1916	Hour	Summary of Events and Information	Remarks and references to Appendices
Hamertinghe	20/1		Lieut. W.R. Keele A.O.D reported for duty, by for instructional duties. MB	
	21/1		On leave.	
	22/1			
	23/1			
	24/1			MB
"	25/1		Returned from leave & absence. General routine. Received new pattern "P.H." gas helmets to replace "P" pattern at rate of one per officer & man.	
	26/1		General Routine & store services.	
	27/1		Proceeded to Armentieres & obtained 1000 rifle covers from Contractor Mr Achille Pogean - Visited 2nd Army Workshops. Ballieul in afternoon to obtain special watches & binoculars.	MB
	28/1		Normal office & store duties. MB	

WAR DIARY
or
INTELLIGENCE SUMMARY

Army Form C. 2118

Place	Date	Hour	Summary of Events and Information	Remarks and references to Appendices
Nieuwkapelle	29/1		Normal store + office duties. Visited 2nd Army Workshops, Poullevil, & obtained opinion of their instruments.	MB
	30/1		Received telegraphic orders to proceed to H.Q. 17th Corps for duty.	MB
	31/1		Handed over duties to Lieut. M.R. Neale, A.O.D.. Left H.Q. 14th Div. to proceed to 17th Corps.	MB

Confidential

— WAR DIARY —

D.A.D.O.S. 14th DIVISION.

1st February to 29th February, 1916.

M Neale Lt. Col.
D.A.D.O.S. 14th Div.

Army Form C. 2118

WAR DIARY
or
INTELLIGENCE SUMMARY
(Erase heading not required.)

Instructions regarding War Diaries and Intelligence Summaries are contained in F.S. Regs., Part II. and the Staff Manual respectively. Title Pages will be prepared in manuscript.

Place	Date 1916	Hour	Summary of Events and Information	Remarks and references to Appendices
Hanebrough	Feb 1		Took over duties from Capt. W. Beckwith who proceeded to 17th Corps	hlR
"	2/2		Normal store and Office duties	hlR
"	3/2		Grant Periscope received	hlR hlR
"	4/2		Visited Hazebrouck and purchased funnels & tubs for Baths	hlR hlR
"	5/2		Normal store and Office duties. Relieved "P" helmets to Base	hlR
"	6/2		Change of Railhead. Visited R.O.O. with view to clearing store prior to move	
"	7/2		Returned quantities of tents and tent-hollows to New Railhead for transmission to Base	hlR
"	8/2		Normal store and Office duties. Arrival of 172 cases of P.H. Helmets. Wired to N. and S. base making arrangements for move.	hlR
"	9/2		Preparations for move out of the area	hlR

1875 Wt. W593/826 1,000,000 4/15 J.B.C. & A. A.D.S.S./Forms/C. 2118.

Army Form C. 2118

WAR DIARY
or
INTELLIGENCE SUMMARY
(Erase heading not required.)

Instructions regarding War Diaries and Intelligence Summaries are contained in F.S. Regs., Part II. and the Staff Manual respectively. Title Pages will be prepared in manuscript.

Place	Date 1916	Hour	Summary of Events and Information	Remarks and references to Appendices
Hamenlinghe	10/2		Visited D.A.D.O.S. 20th Div at Eyguelbeco, and made arrangements to take over his Dumps and Offices.	nil
	11/2		Visit of D.A.D.O.S. 20th Div to inspect 2nd Army area dump, and a run taking over same.	nil
	12/2		Change of ordnance to Railhead. Transferred from Northern to Southern Base.	nil
	13/2		Handed over certain area stores to D.A.D.O.S. 20th Div.	nil
Eyguelbec			Departed from Hamenlinghe for Eyguelbec, arriving this same day.	nil
	14/2		New Railhead established at Aruche. Transferred to 2nd Army.	nil
	15/2		Attended refilling points at Hamelincke, Heemzeele, and Jaggeo Capperulle.	nil
	16/2		Usual office duties	nil
	17/2		Normal duties	nil
	18/2		Preparations for removal to Hessels	nil
Hessels	19/2		Established a Dump at Hessels	nil
	20/2		Visited new railhead at Caela.	nil
	21/2		Attended refilling points at Hessels, and St Chausia	nil

WAR DIARY
or
INTELLIGENCE SUMMARY

(Erase heading not required.)

Army Form C. 2118

(3)

Place	Date	Hour	Summary of Events and Information	Remarks and references to Appendices
Heads	22/2		Normal routine.	MR
	23/2		Visited 3rd Army Heavy Mobile Workshops at Beauval.	MR
Doullens	24/2		Left 2 cwwk for Doullens at two hours notice. Took over stores on termes handed over back to S.A.D.S. 3rd Div. Parked lorries in Doullens for the night.	MR
	25/2		Left Doullens for Sus St Leger. Heavy snowstorm and roads very difficult. No news of stores being sent to Achiet-le-Petit.	MR
Sus St	26/2		Roads snowed up. No news of stores being units ordered to village.	MR
Leger				
"	27/2		Visited new Railhead at Saulty. Drivers scattered. Lorries stone difficult. Arranged to draw acc stores from Railhead on the 29th inst.	MR
	28/2		Kept Sus St Leger for Barly. No storage available. Found store in Saulty village moved stores in from Station. Artillery pouch at Station.	MR
	29/2			MR

All made country roads

DADOS
14 D W
Vol 1D

CONFIDENTIAL

WAR DIARY

DADOS 14th DIVISION

FOR

MARCH 1916
MAR. 1st — MAR. 31st

M. Healey.
K.O.D.
D.A.D.O.S.

Army Form C. 2118

WAR DIARY
or
INTELLIGENCE SUMMARY

(Erase heading not required.)

Instructions regarding War Diaries and Intelligence Summaries are contained in F. S. Regs., Part II. and the Staff Manual respectively. Title Pages will be prepared in manuscript.

Place	Date 1916	Hour	Summary of Events and Information	Remarks and references to Appendices
Barly	1/3		Unit proceeded as usual. Refilling point paid at Toutencourt	nil
	2/3		Visited store at Sailly and refilling point at Toutencourt	nil
	3/3		Visited Bonneville to find site and offices. No store yet available	nil
	4/3		Moved Office to Bonneville.	nil
	5/3		Normal routine and office duties	nil
Bonneville	6/3		Normal routine and office duties.	nil
	7/3		Distribution of trench stores	nil
	8/3		Established store at Bonneville.	nil
	9/3		Lorries engaged with transit of stores from Sailly to Bonneville	nil
	9/3		Refilling point discontinued. Units requested to attend at store.	nil
	10/3		Normal routine and office duties	nil
	11/3		Visited out-lying store at Warlus. Sent Pte William to Photo School at Beauzegneaux A.O.C	nil

1875 Wt. W593/826 1,000,000 4/15 J.B.C. & A. A.D.S.S./Forms/C. 2118.

WAR DIARY
or
INTELLIGENCE SUMMARY

(Erase heading not required.)

Army Form C. 2118

Place	Date	Hour	Summary of Events and Information	Remarks and references to Appendices
Beauville	12/3		Visited Doullens to purchase rope. Obtained but of available shops for local purchases.	n/R
	13/3		Normal duties in dump and office.	n/R
	14/3		Normal duties in dump and office.	n/R
	15/3		Arranged to take suitable dump at Warlus	n/R
WARLUS	16/3		Established dump at WARLUS — farm buildings, bie office and available yard at rear.	n/R
	17/3		Appendicitis outbreak owing to him arriving during middle day, and departing same evening at Railhead.	n/R
	18/3			
	19/3		Normal duties in store and office.	n/R
	20/3			

Army Form C. 2118

WAR DIARY
or
INTELLIGENCE SUMMARY
(Erase heading not required.)

Instructions regarding War Diaries and Intelligence Summaries are contained in F. S. Regs., Part II. and the Staff Manual respectively. Title Pages will be prepared in manuscript.

Place	Date	Hour	Summary of Events and Information	Remarks and references to Appendices
WARLUS	1916			
	21/3		Both established and units directed to send all units/supplies to Bdr discussion with A.D.M.S. as to possibilities of placing are control of same. Quarterclothing with O/C Bath	M.R.
	22/3		Normal routine. Stated use of narrow gauge railway from SMULTY	M.R.
	23/3		to WANQUETIN. Re establishment of Divisional Ammunition Obsp. As ammunis. withdrawn from Bdes for the purpose	M.R.
	24/3		Inspected various wagons spents and reported any defects of axles, and had brakes to Transport Officers concerned.	M.R.
	25/3			M.R.
	26/3		Normal duties	M.R.
	27/3			M.R.
	28/3		Returns sent to Corps. of Personnel and Lewis Gun baggage.	M.R.
	29/3		Normal duties and preparation of quarterly Budh return to	
	30/3		Army	M.R.
	31/3			

DADOS
14 Div
Vol II

M. Kendel
D.A.D.O.S.
14 Div.

WAR DIARY.

April 1st – April 30th
1916.

D.A.D.O.S. 14th Div.

CONFIDENTIAL.

Army Form C. 2118

WAR DIARY
or
INTELLIGENCE SUMMARY
(Erase heading not required.)

Instructions regarding War Diaries and Intelligence Summaries are contained in F. S. Regs., Part II. and the Staff Manual respectively. Title Pages will be prepared in manuscript.

Place	Date	Hour	Summary of Events and Information	Remarks and references to Appendices
WARLUS 1916	1/4		Moved Office and store duties	hRh
	2/4		Quarterly Batt. return prepared and sent, where form to have been. Excuse in demands, weather for preparation	hRh
	3/4		39th Anti Aircraft Section apply for Advance Store Apparently not clear as to where originally filed, due to change of Officers. Proceed to interview A.D.O.S. Corps as to method of administration	hRh
	4/4		Arrival of Tower Box Respirators. Issue made. Rank in front line position and likely to be exposed to gas attacks	hRh
	5/4		Units being in French stores collected from billets. List made and sent to A.A.Q.M.G. 14 Division for instructions for disposal.	hRh
	6/4		Endeavour made to obtain a sling for Lewis Guns for use in trenches.	hRh
	7/4		Report from S.D.6. Division to this sample oblg.	hRh
	8/4		Arrival of food containers for hind work.	hRh

WAR DIARY
INTELLIGENCE SUMMARY
(Erase heading not required.)

Army Form C. 2118

Place	Date	Hour	Summary of Events and Information	Remarks and references to Appendices
WARLUS	9/4		Number of bulged barrels returned from units. As these completely damaged rifle request made to units for explanation. Bulged barrel rifles returned	
	10/4		to units for General Insp'n. Lbd. trains also inspected. Finds these Several Batts made to that units do not return unfixed for cleaning. G.R.O. issued on the subject	
	11/4		Distribution of Rifle amongst new units	
	12/4			
	13/4		Issue of experimental bombers shields to units Issue of Mills light rifle dischr. to units	
	14/4		Normal Office duties	
	15/4		New pat. Stove Lett. arrived for Bde. hd.qrs. Bn. Batteries. Units instructed to pass to Ordnance surplus stores & ask for new items	
	16/4			
	17/4		Normal routine	

WAR DIARY
or
INTELLIGENCE SUMMARY

(Erase heading not required.)

Army Form C. 2118

Place	Date	Hour	Summary of Events and Information	Remarks and references to Appendices
MARLUS	18/4		Visited R.O.O. 7th Corps and pointed out difficulties of transport on the narrow gauge railway, & promised to report this.	/n/h
	19/4		Visited ARRAS and met Lou hays, he is to try & transport for whom stores would be purchased.	/n/h
	20/4		The wagons ordered from Base for General Rest camps	/n/h
	21/4		Authority given for 3rd Army to purchase shells and rifles for Sailors' Shop	/n/h
	22/4		Armourer sent out from workshops to inspect rifles of unit	/n/h
	23/4		Workshop shed ordered in district, students not responsible if sent in order to prevent duplication.	/n/h
	24/4		Visited GZZDS 38' gun. Normal duties in office	/n/h
	25/4		Information received of arrival of 15" Lator Bell (16"6m) from the General area. Visited the unit & found this very badly fitted, have arranged supply one of the most necessary items	/n/h

Army Form C. 2118

WAR DIARY or INTELLIGENCE SUMMARY

(Erase heading not required.)

Place	Date	Hour	Summary of Events and Information	Remarks and references to Appendices
NYERI	26/4		Two of J.I.A.D.O's SB' Gun not now to today over Depot. Issue of 50 rifles taken by instruction of A.D.O.S. 6th Batn.	hfh
	27/4		Opened Shoemaker's Shop with four men to prepare & repair boots for units with no shoemaker.	hfh
	28/4		9 D.M. 6th Batn. inspn. that no more rifles can be dealt with by him until further notice own to present front.	hfh
	29/4		Arrival of new reserve of P.H. Smoke helmets — one per officer and man. then now open at question of canvas during move etc., in possession of four lorries.	hfh
	30/4		Normal duties — Nyeri and store	hfh

Confidential

DADOS
14 D3
Vol. 12

WAR DIARY

May 1st – 31st 1916

D.A.D.O.S.
14 DIV.

M. Heale
Capt
SADOS
14 Div

Army Form C. 2118

WAR DIARY
or
INTELLIGENCE SUMMARY
(Erase heading not required.)

Instructions regarding War Diaries and Intelligence Summaries are contained in F. S. Regs., Part II. and the Staff Manual respectively. Title Pages will be prepared in manuscript.

Place	Date	Hour	Summary of Events and Information	Remarks and references to Appendices
WARLUS	1/5		Normal duties in Store and offices. Return of Rags Horse	nil
	2/5		Return of blankets, clothing and just blankets for men came very heavy pressure on owner staff and transport	nil
	3/5		Stoneman with Hyn Sow as Kmer of Tailors Shop and decision to establish same. Went to ARRAS for purchase of materials for same.	nil
	4/5		Experimental canvas for Lewis trappers in trenches prepared for inspection by G.O.C. 6th Div. sent trench troubles to I.O.M 6th Corps. nil	nil
	5/5		Normal duties — Store and Offices	nil
	6/5		Move of 24th "J" Inf. Bde entailing re-arrangement of sanitary details as hitherto soil pith a site working.	nil
	7/5		Establishment of Tailors Shop. Change of railhead to TINQUES.	nil
	8/5		Normal duties	nil

WAR DIARY or INTELLIGENCE SUMMARY

Army Form C. 2118

(Erase heading not required.)

Place	Date	Hour	Summary of Events and Information	Remarks and references to Appendices
WARLUS	9/5		Notice given to units of summer scale of clothing to begin 15th inst	MBh
	10/5		Enquiry instituted as to large number of items of clothing demanded by units. This was pointed out to BCos. who promised to take up the matter with units.	MBh
	11/5		Experimental bins being made, to hold 6 Lewis Gun magazines, by construction of S.O.C.	MBh
	12/5		Normal duties.	MBh
	13/5		Normal duties.	MBh
	14/5		Visited A&Q/G LM Bnty reference damaged gun (Stokes Gun)	MBh
	15/5		Subject of Requisition taken up with Division, but cannot now to make Requisitions without authority from Bde. Hqrs. Royl. service concerned	MBh
	16/5		Normal duties ~ After store.	MBh

Army Form C. 2118

WAR DIARY
or
INTELLIGENCE SUMMARY

(Erase heading not required.)

Instructions regarding War Diaries and Intelligence Summaries are contained in F. S. Regs., Part II. and the Staff Manual respectively. Title Pages will be prepared in manuscript.

Place	Date	Hour	Summary of Events and Information	Remarks and references to Appendices
WARLUS	17/5		Visit to Town MAJOR ARRAS on subject of requisitions	
	18/5		Arranged to have our mi'hundred set of underclothing to 41° Brigade in order to establish Baths whilst out of divisional area.	
	19/5		Normal duties	
	20/5		The III Army heavy mobile workshops taken on a growth of repaired wheels. This arrangement the public will save time as all wheels formerly came up from Base.	
	21/5		Shewed other wounts to personnel on prevention of fires in the stove and billets.	
	22/5		Normal duties	
	23/5		Normal duties	
	24/5		Alteration of Artillery formation and receipt of spare barrows Gens of Bde Machine Gun Company	
	25/5		Overhauling machine Guns of Armourers Shop	

1875 Wt. W593/826 1,000,000 4/15 J.B.C. & A. A.D.S.S./Forms/C.2118.

Army Form C. 2118

WAR DIARY
or
INTELLIGENCE SUMMARY

(Erase heading not required.)

Instructions regarding War Diaries and Intelligence Summaries are contained in F. S. Regs., Part II. and the Staff Manual respectively. Title Pages will be prepared in manuscript.

Place	Date	Hour	Summary of Events and Information	Remarks and references to Appendices
MARLES	26/5		Experimental boat carrying Ben Trade up of Ships at interview of C.O.S.	with
	27/5		Arranged to have Gas helmets inspected by Anti-Gas School expert each week so that no faulty cases of such may be made	with
			Removed rifle point for 41°Cdy Bn to ACO.	with
	28/5		LADDS departed on leave	with
	29/5			
	30/5		C.O. i/c charge reported Normal office duties	with
	31/5			

1875 Wt. W593/826 1,000,000 4/15 J.B.C. & A. A.D.S.S./Forms/C. 2118.

DADOS 14.Div
Vol 13 June

WAR DIARY.

June 1st — June 30th
1916.

D.A.D.O.S.
14.Div.

CONFIDENTIAL.

H. Kealer
D.A.D.O.S.
14 Div.

Army Form C. 2118

WAR DIARY
or
INTELLIGENCE SUMMARY

(Erase heading not required.)

Instructions regarding War Diaries and Intelligence Summaries are contained in F. S. Regs., Part II. and the Staff Manual respectively. Title Pages will be prepared in manuscript.

Place	Date	Hour	Summary of Events and Information	Remarks and references to Appendices
MARLUS	1/6			
	2/6		S.A.D.T.S. on leave	
	3/6		I.O. in charge reported Normal office duties	App.
	4/6			
	5/6			
	6/6			
	7/6			
	8/6		Normal duties	App.
	9/6		Local purchasing at AVEIGNES.	App.
	10/6		Visited ARRAS to purchase machine for tailor shop	App.
	11/6		Arrival of Inspector of Armourers, First Army	App.
	12/6		Visit of D.D.T.S. III Army. Despatched first consignment of Lewis magazines to Heavy Mobile Workshop for modification of lock spring	App.

1875 W. W593/826 1,000,000 4/15 J.B.C. & A. A.D.S.S./Forms/C. 2118.

Army Form C. 2118

WAR DIARY
or
INTELLIGENCE SUMMARY

(Erase heading not required.)

Instructions regarding War Diaries and Intelligence Summaries are contained in F.S. Regs., Part II. and the Staff Manual respectively. Title Pages will be prepared in manuscript.

Place	Date	Hour	Summary of Events and Information	Remarks and references to Appendices
WARLUS	13/6		Normal duties in Office and Store.	
"	14/6		Received contribution from S.O.G. to procure as many items to arm of	
"	15/6		3 pm MrIn man for purpose of fastening smoke labels. Normal duties	
"	16/6		Issue of one day's specimen made of Browning Clips for and Lewis Guns to Armourers	
"	17/6		Receipt from 3rd Army of Army trench booklet of trench cart	
"	18/6		Receipt & issue of Lewis Gun magazines for mountings to Armourers	
"	19/6		Normal Office & store routine	
"	20/6			
"	21/6		Visit to Antique School reference the examination of ace PH. helmets has returned "burnt" as released consequent to wear of PH6	
"	22/6			
"	23/6		Normal duties.	
"	24/6			

Army Form C. 2118

WAR DIARY
or
INTELLIGENCE SUMMARY
(Erase heading not required.)

Instructions regarding War Diaries and Intelligence Summaries are contained in F. S. Regs., Part II. and the Staff Manual respectively. Title Pages will be prepared in manuscript.

Place	Date	Hour	Summary of Events and Information	Remarks and references to Appendices
WARLUS	25/6		Visit of A.D.S. Vi Corps who gave instructions to issue further Tunnelling bags and one blanket per man	hJR
"	26/6		Preparations being made for Special dumps - Case of advance	hJR
"	27/6		5th Wilts. Battl. ask permission to make a smoke dump of clothes. This was refused, being contrary to instructions to units - the field	hJR
"	28/6		Normal duties	hJR
"	30/6		Preparation of Corps howh: return of slam dem.dep from Base	hJR

1875 Wt. W593/826 1,000,000 4/15 J.B.C. & A. A.D.S.S./Forms/C. 2118.

14/ Vol 14 / July 8

WAR DIARY.

D.A.D.O.S 14th Div.

July 1st – 31st 1916.

CONFIDENTIAL.

M. Keulefer
L.n.D.t
14th

Army Form C. 2118

WAR DIARY
or
INTELLIGENCE SUMMARY
(Erase heading not required.)

Place	Date	Hour	Summary of Events and Information	Remarks and references to Appendices
MARLUS	1/7/16		Set up dump of Div'l Details with Third Army S.D.O.T. personnel to expedite issues. List of outstanding figures sent to S.D.O.T.	nil
	2/7/16		Normal duties — Office and dump.	
	3/7/16		Arranged to take over unspent stores from 5th Div S.A.D.O.T. moving out. Return of Lewis Gun magazines from units received. Figures visible by O.C. did not agree with ordnance records. Arranged with D.A.D.O.S. Division to go into differences with representatives of various units concerned. Lewis gun magazines had to be reissued at Third Army Hqrs mobile workshop, but three S/Sgt Armourers to assist.	
	4/7/16			
	5/7/16		5" Div dump established at GRAND ROULECOURT. Stores of equipment taken over from the dumps & now with the Div.	
	6/7/16		Received weakness in structure of Trench Mortar had arisen – have Pins & block repaired at Corps workshop.	

Army Form C. 2118

WAR DIARY
or
INTELLIGENCE SUMMARY

(Erase heading not required.)

Instructions regarding War Diaries and Intelligence Summaries are contained in F.S. Regs., Part II. and the Staff Manual respectively. Title Pages will be prepared in manuscript.

Place	Date	Hour	Summary of Events and Information	Remarks and references to Appendices
WARLUS	7/5/26	p.m.	Inspection of Iron Rations & Personnel. Reported to Bn Hqrs all correct.	
	8/5/26		Officer's arms met R.O.O. Reallent over mittent of clothing of dispatch of old clothing from Salvage Co. to Railhead. Gave instructions to Salvage men as to correct method of dispatch.	
	9/5/26		Vickers Gun notifiers as being sent by train from ABBEVILLE to Railhead for 8th M.M.G. Co. Delays on the road.	
	10/5/26		7 – 3.75" Trench mortars sent to Third Army Trench Mortar School. O.C. T.M. School regrets/information of the eighth Trench mortar. Information given that this was sent to Base at the end of June, being rendered unserviceable by shell fire.	
	11/5/26		Normal duties	
	12/5/26		Normal duties	

WAR DIARY or INTELLIGENCE SUMMARY

Army Form C. 2118

Place	Date	Hour	Summary of Events and Information	Remarks and references to Appendices
MARLES	13/9/16		Question arose as to charge of levy small pox holes in new Smoke Helmets. Reference made to Anti Gas Expert who reported that to be of little importance. Departure of Corps. Holland for Base.	
	14/9/16		Arrival of S/Sgt Naith from 56th Div. S.A.D.T.S. Shortage of G.S. paint heavy upon the div. Unit pressed for more. Visit of L.D.V.S. this day. Put up question of paint shortage. Visit of A.D.V.S who regrets that assistance should be given to 11th Div. just arriving in the V. Corps.	
	15/9/16		Normal duties	
	16/9/16		Visits D.A.D.V.S. 11th Div. with view to giving any possible assistance.	
	17/9/16		Units already keen number of underclothing, and stating that clothing was sent from hands in a satisfactory manner at laundry. Visited Laundry and made arrangements with O.C. Baths to provide	P.T.O

Army Form C. 2118

WAR DIARY
or
INTELLIGENCE SUMMARY
(Erase heading not required.)

Instructions regarding War Diaries and Intelligence Summaries are contained in F. S. Regs., Part II. and the Staff Manual respectively. Title Pages will be prepared in manuscript.

Place	Date	Hour	Summary of Events and Information	Remarks and references to Appendices
WAREUS	17/7/16		(continued) Larger quantities of soap & soda; and also to augment the shirts at the Laundry.	
	18/7/16		Normal duties.	
	19/7/16		Visit of D.D.O.S. Division and A.D.O.S this Army. Inspection of Divisional Workshops.	
	20/7/16		Various Anti Gas School on gravitee of air another fabric being examined by Expert before issue to units of the Division.	
	21/7/16		Systematic perusal of indents & indenting intents of are emit not kept in Ordnance or Q.M. Dept. Such units are greatly confused by various authorities and need persistent roots and personal checks over & all outstanding indents.	
	22/7/16		Special Lewis Gun magazine buckets being manufactured — the forward workshops here on extra time. 500 made up to ace.	

Army Form C. 2118

WAR DIARY
or
INTELLIGENCE SUMMARY
(Erase heading not required.)

Instructions regarding War Diaries and Intelligence Summaries are contained in F.S. Regs., Part II. and the Staff Manual respectively. Title Pages will be prepared in manuscript.

Place	Date	Hour	Summary of Events and Information	Remarks and references to Appendices
WARLUS	23/7/16		Visited 9. OM & Corp. Took Lewis Bren mechanism and pointed out weakness. He promised to strengthen any future mechanisms brought to from units.	
	24/7/16		Visit of D.A.D.O.S. 21° Div.in who reported none of underclothing shirts nothing was found to be available.	
	25/7/16		normal duties	
	26/7/16		normal duties.	
	27/7/16		Equipment of V/14 Heavy T.M Battery begun	
	28/7/16		normal duties	
	29/7/16		Preparation for departure from area	
	30/7/16		Hauled our Lewis & central stores to L.A.D.O.S 11" Div. Proceeded to SUS S' LEGER.	
	31/7/16		Began refitting front teeth as GRAND ROOLECOURT.	

14 / Vol 15

Contracted   WAR DIARY

D.A.D.O.S.
14 Div.

August 1st
to
August 31st. 1916

M. Keale Lt.

Army Form C. 2118

WAR DIARY
or
INTELLIGENCE SUMMARY
(Erase heading not required.)

Instructions regarding War Diaries and Intelligence Summaries are contained in F.S. Regs., Part II. and the Staff Manual respectively. Title Pages will be prepared in manuscript.

Place	Date 1916	Hour	Summary of Events and Information	Remarks and references to Appendices
ROUEN. LE GRAND	1/8/16		43rd Res. M.9. Co. report apparently with transport. Inspected vehicles and obtained new London Books.	[initials]
BERNEVILLE	2/8/16		Arrived at BERNEVILLE. Reported at HAUTEVILLE for instructions. These units have been left in the ARRAS district.	
"	3/8/16		Purchased quantity of washing and wringing machines for 1st Corps Laundry being established at ST. OUEN.	
"	4/8/16		Visited ADS1 IX Corps with AA. QMG on following:— 1. Been of Steel Helmets. really more satisfactory 2. Shortage of handcarts for French troops. 6. Entire lack of horse drawn handcarts. Second French Division from Base for their own.	
"	5/8/16		Normal duties	
"	6/8/16		Moved to BUIRE. Petrol & dump near Railway line on BUIRE-TREUX Railway.	HEILLY

1875 Wt. W593/826 1,000,000 4/15 J.B.C. & A. A.D.S.S./Forms/C. 2118.

Army Form C. 2118

WAR DIARY
or
INTELLIGENCE SUMMARY
(Erase heading not required.)

Instructions regarding War Diaries and Intelligence Summaries are contained in F. S. Regs., Part II. and the Staff Manual respectively. Title Pages will be prepared in manuscript.

Place	Date	Hour	Summary of Events and Information	Remarks and references to Appendices
BURE	7/8/16		Normal duties	
	8/8/16		Visited ADOS XV Corps and reported shortage of Steel Helmets and Lanyards. Received and sent consignment instructions to take all repairs to return to No. 17 obsp.	
	9/8/16			
	10/8/16		Now ammunitioning 5 Siege Artillery	
	11/8/16		Called to see French mortar Blewitt Sight for re-adjustment	
	12/8/16		Normal duties	
ALBERT	13/8/16		Moved to BELLE-VUE-FARM. Pitched a dump on the ALBERT road. Received authority from Fourth Army for one marquee	
	14/8/16		Arrange to supply stores to 17th Div Artillery if necessary	
	15/8/16		Based 17 Div leaving the area. Instructions for G Coach truck Special Signal Sheet - these consist of black cloth background 10ft × 7ft on which black capital letter 3ft sheet wide.	

WAR DIARY
or
INTELLIGENCE SUMMARY
(Erase heading not required.)

Army Form C. 2118

Place	Date 1916	Hour	Summary of Events and Information	Remarks and references to Appendices
ALBERT	16/8/16		Normal duties	
	17/8/16		Found it very necessary to keep Lewis guns & oil covered for snipers during heavy artillery bombardment	
	18/8/16		Normal duties	
	19/8/16		Artillery endeavoured to take guns out of action to G.O.M.	
			Batteries found to be enough fitters remaining out of group arranged to have acc 18pdr group sent to G.O.M.	
	20/8/16		Normal duties	
	21/8/16		17" R.A. and part of 5" R.A. came over	
	22/8/16		Heavy demands for machine guns, clothing and oil	
	23/8/16		Special signalling class completed and issued	
	24/8/16		Repaired three Lewis Guns & slips	

WAR DIARY
or
INTELLIGENCE SUMMARY

(Erase heading not required.)

Army Form C. 2118

Place	Date	Hour	Summary of Events and Information	Remarks and references to Appendices
ALBERT	25/8/16		Visited by O.C. Reinforcements who stated apparently ill re-equipping men out of hospital and down there. Promised to provide uniform for the purpose.	
"	26/8/16		as BURE horned ambln	
"	27/8/16		41° Sup Bee withdrawn from the line made a systematic foot-wash and commenced to re-equip. Baths arranged at YMCA Hut and clean clothing out for each man.	
"	28/8/16		Issue of clothing continuing to 41° Bee	
"	29/8/16		Arranged to overhaul French horses of 41" DM Battery	
"	30/8/16		Handed over 10.080 Souch Nebosh Exposh by inoculation 8 SAI OMG	
"	31/8/16		Moved from ALBERT to BELLOY ST LEONARD	

Confidential

vol 16

WAR DIARY

D.A.D.O.S.

1st Div.

Sept 1 - 1916
Sept 30 - 1916

h. Heule Capt.
DADOS
1st Div.

Army Form C. 2118

WAR DIARY
or
INTELLIGENCE SUMMARY
(Erase heading not required.)

Instructions regarding War Diaries and Intelligence Summaries are contained in F.S. Regs., Part II. and the Staff Manual respectively. Title Pages will be prepared in manuscript.

Place	Date	Hour	Summary of Events and Information	Remarks and references to Appendices
BELLOY S.^T LEONARD	1/9/16		Railhead at HENGEST. Arrival of 5 Kitchens. Difficulty in removing stores due to want of transport. This difficulty always arises on the move due to fact of having to reconvoy stores from the railhead twice in a day of departure and also to the inability of R.O.O's stores truck pending arrival at new for move this one day.	
	2/9/16		Transferred administration of 14th Bir. Artillery to 24th Div. D.A.D.O.S. Established shops at HENGEST.	
	3/9/16		Issued clean underclothing to 42nd Bee Baths at HORNOY. Arranged with 42nd Bee to issue underclothing trench direct for a few days due to delay in erection of Baths.	
	4/9/16		Command line of units of 42nd Bde. with a view to looking their equipment. Found T. Mortar Battery short of carts. To 17/H I can not available. Repairs come intact to Div.	
	5/9/16		Visits A.D.O.S. F. Corps. Reported need of 28 Lewis Gun Carts and 20,000 steel helmets. Arranged to draw from C.O. Corps troops a large supply of socks and shirts.	

WAR DIARY
or
INTELLIGENCE SUMMARY

(Erase heading not required.)

Army Form C. 2118

Place	Date 1916	Hour	Summary of Events and Information	Remarks and references to Appendices
BELLOY	6/9/16		Normal duties.	
	7/9/16		Report from 9" R.B. that type of handle provided for Lewis Gun carriers weak at point where it joins the cart. Demands new wheels. Pointed out the weakness in transferring to L.O.M. IX Corps who arranged to strengthen handle. Issued instructions traced accordingly.	
	8/9/16			
	9/9/16		Information of early move from Divisional H.Qrs. Notification of arrival of transport vehicles at Raillies. Arrangts to use same as reserve vehicles by agreement with units.	
	10/9/16		Moved dump by rail and lorry to point at junction of ALBERT-MEAULTE roads.	
	11/9/16		Moved office to BUIRE. RAILHEAD at HEILLY.	
BUIRE	12/9/16		Raillies changed to ALBERT. Reports urgent requirement of steel helmets to ADOS XV Corps. hired R.O.D's as salvage Necun for same.	

WAR DIARY
or
INTELLIGENCE SUMMARY

(Erase heading not required.)

Army Form C. 2118

Place	Date 1916	Hour	Summary of Events and Information	Remarks and references to Appendices
BUIRE	13/9/16		Moved Office to dump. Hqrs. Division moved to TRICOURT. Units urgently demanding Steel helmets and rifles. Received consignment of 150 steel helmets from BASE. Number of steel helmets with unit from salvage and nothing.	
	14/9/16		Preparation of Special Particulars made re Tachir Clerp for carriage of Walei kits in case of absence.	
	15/9/16		Bde. hinckpots made to draw stores due to Sudden order to move up. Arranged Whole stores for a few days during advance and to carry at refilling point as required.	
	16/9/16		Normal duties.	
	17/9/16		Moved Hq. Office to BUIRE. Units come out of the line. Unit to remain in same place.	
BUIRE	18/9/16		Units very short of all equipment. Commenced issuing units of 4" Bde. (wire) for all machine guns to replace lost or unserviceable.	

A.D.M.S. XIV Corps Field Group.

Army Form C. 2118

WAR DIARY
or
INTELLIGENCE SUMMARY
(Erase heading not required.)

Instructions regarding War Diaries and Intelligence Summaries are contained in F. S. Regs., Part II. and the Staff Manual respectively. Title Pages will be prepared in manuscript.

Place	Date	Hour	Summary of Events and Information	Remarks and references to Appendices
BOIRE	1916 19/9		Commenced to re-equip 4D Bac Units.	
	20/9		Filled up bottles and undercloths. Report called for on to disposal of oxy-acetylene Plants whilst area in possession of R.E. Companies. Report sent to Fourth Army that all were sent to Base.	
	21/9		Charge of Base. Move of Division announced. Selected new group at LE CAUROY. Sent N trailer & stores to units direct due to heavy dublin lorry, otherwise carried out by unit own transport.	
LE CAUROY	22/9		Sqn move to LE CAUROY. Horses drunk. Norfuis Base. Left 1 Corpl 1 L/cpl and 3 men to administer R.S.A. units of 1st Div. Established a Wkn for the section at HEILLY. Norfuis XV Corps.	

WAR DIARY
INTELLIGENCE SUMMARY

Army Form C. 2118

Place	Date	Hour	Summary of Events and Information	Remarks and references to Appendices
LE CAUROY	23/9		Reported arrival in person to ADOS VI Corps. Noticed means that 12 Bn as well as 33" Div. artillery were to be allotted for Ordnance Duties. Reported that the work would be too heavy. Saw ADOS who regretted that no other plan was practicable.	
	24/9/16		Normal duties.	
	25/9/16		Normal duties.	
	26/9		Divisional Hqrs. move to GOUY. Established office in GOUY.	
	27/9		Normal duties.	
	29/9		Took over Dump at WARLUS for 12" Div. Also aee [?] units of 12 Div. artillery as well as Bde of 33" Artillery.	

WAR DIARY
or
INTELLIGENCE SUMMARY
(Erase heading not required.)

Army Form C. 2118

Place	Date	Hour	Summary of Events and Information	Remarks and references to Appendices
NAPLES	29/9		Began issue of stores to all attacks units. Receive two loads of stores from SA.00.7 33" Bn. for unit of that Bn.	
			Extra work very heavy.	
			Also began issue of field P.H.G. helmet for men	
			Also began issue of one blanket per man.	
	30/9		Continuation of above issues. Visited Ordnance Decline admin [?]. 14 R.A at NEUILLY. Arranged to transfer from XI Corps to VI Corps	
			Also to refit on the way up at LUCHEUX.	

Vol 17

"CONFIDENTIAL"

WAR DIARY.

D.A.D.O.S.
14th DIV.

Oct. 1st – Oct 31st
1916

M. Heale (or)
DADMS
14 Div

Army Form C. 2118

WAR DIARY
or
INTELLIGENCE SUMMARY
(Erase heading not required.)

Instructions regarding War Diaries and Intelligence Summaries are contained in F.S. Regs., Part II. and the Staff Manual respectively. Title Pages will be prepared in manuscript.

Place	Date	Hour	Summary of Events and Information	Remarks and references to Appendices
WARLUS	1/10		Normal work in DUMP. Units 14 Div R.A. still detached but on the way to rejoin—today at TALMAS. Replies at TALMAS. Seemed that 2 guns outstanding. Arranged Advance details relative to change of establishment from four to six gun batteries.	
	2/10		D.D.O.S. That Army Mobile DUMP. Instructions received that the mobile would be sent to PRESENT. Stated that Salvage dump above to new Ordnance	
	3/10		Normal duties	
	4/10		Visit paid by A.D.O.S. V Corps. Different methods of keeping stock took under discussion.	
	5/10		Transferred units of 33 Div. to D.A.D.O.S. 49 Div.	
	6/10		Reorganised Franklin of stores to 49 Div.	
	7/10		Normal duties.	

Army Form C. 2118

WAR DIARY
or
INTELLIGENCE SUMMARY

(Erase heading not required.)

Instructions regarding War Diaries and Intelligence Summaries are contained in F.S. Regs., Part II. and the Staff Manual respectively. Title Pages will be prepared in manuscript.

Place	Date	Hour	Summary of Events and Information	Remarks and references to Appendices
WARLUS	8/10		Received hire guns for 14th R.A.	
	9/10		Arrangement made with Staff Capt and 2.O.M to fit ballistic caps guns due from Base.	
			Despatch of special stores to A/c Laundry in preparation of start of Divisional Laundry.	
			Receipt of special Picture Gun for 8th M.M.G. Co.	
	10/10		Leave granted to D.A.D.O.S from morning 9 / 11th inst.	
	11/10		L.A. D.D.S departed on leave.	
	12/10		Normal Office duties	
	13/10		Builder a hut for personnel	
	14/10		Normal duties	
	15/10		Normal duties	

Army Form C. 2118

WAR DIARY
or
INTELLIGENCE SUMMARY
(Erase heading not required.)

Instructions regarding War Diaries and Intelligence Summaries are contained in F. S. Regs., Part II. and the Staff Manual respectively. Title Pages will be prepared in manuscript.

Place	Date	Hour	Summary of Events and Information	Remarks and references to Appendices
WARLUS	16/10		Obtained special cattle carriers from Corps for carriage of Trench Mortar Ammunition.	
	17/10		Normal duties	
	18/10		Normal duties	
	19/10		Normal duties	
	20/10		L/C L.O.T. returned from leave	
	21/10		Notice of proposed move of Division	
	22/10		Visit of D.A.D.O.S. 12 Div and arrangements made to hand over.	
	23/10		Arrival of unit store of rugs horse.	
	24/10		Verbal L.O.T. This Army and Divn authority for demand of 50 Ranges Oliver	

1875 W+ W 593/826 1,000,000 4/15 J.B.C. & A. A.D.S.S./Forms/C. 2118.

WAR DIARY
or
INTELLIGENCE SUMMARY

(Erase heading not required.)

Army Form C. 2118

Place	Date	Hour	Summary of Events and Information	Remarks and references to Appendices
WARLUS	1916 25/10		Mains dump at LE CAUROY. Issued notice to R.A, R.E. and Pioneers that a refilling point would be made for their units owing to temporary delay in the S.A. are. ace other units to follow new dump then to take effect from 27" inst.	
	26/10		Arrival of I.A.D.O.S. 12 Div. Commenced handing over. Checked off spare stores to new dump.	
LE CAUROY	27/10		Dump moved to LE CAUROY. Refit held at WARLUS for Artillery and attached units.	
	28/10		Visited D.O.M reference state of guns and howitzers. Received large consignments of leather jerkins. Issued horse rugs to Div. Cavalry units' transport.	
	29/10		Held refilling for Artillery and attached units at WANQUETIN - FOSSEUX road at 11.0 A.M. Issued issue of stores at LE CAUROY. Held overview from above to exchange S.M.R.R. rifles.	

D 1875 Wt. W593/826 1,000,000 4/15 J.B.C.& A. A.D.S.S./Forms/C. 2118.

Army Form C. 2118

WAR DIARY
or
INTELLIGENCE SUMMARY
(Erase heading not required.)

Instructions regarding War Diaries and Intelligence Summaries are contained in F. S. Regs., Part II. and the Staff Manual respectively. Title Pages will be prepared in manuscript.

Place	Date	Hour	Summary of Events and Information	Remarks and references to Appendices
LE CAUROY	30/10		Arrival of further consignment of underclothing and 1800 gloves arrived from Boves. Experience great difficulty in dealing with heavy and large quantities of winter clothing. Asked Division for more transport.	
	31/10		Issue of underclothing to Artillery units at no 30 arm & infantry point moved down to other units — the dump	

M. Henderson
Capt.
1st Div

1875 Wt. W593/826 1,000,000 4/15 J.B.C. & A. A.D.S.S./Forms/C. 2118.

Vol 18

WAR DIARY.
Nov 1st – 30th
1916.

D.A.D.O.S.
14 DIV.

Confidential

WAR DIARY
or
INTELLIGENCE SUMMARY

(Erase heading not required.)

Army Form C. 2118

Place	Date	Hour	Summary of Events and Information	Remarks and references to Appendices
Nov 1916				
LE CAUROY	1/11		Artillery repair at WANQUETIN.	
	2/11		Issue of arms flasks for men to commence	
	3/11		Normal duties	
	4/11		Employed loading by unit as to Garlick's 8 phosphor bangs. Went to Gas Cylinder of fresh teams	
	5/11		Sent ample damaged cylinders to L.O.M 17 Corps	
	6/11		Normal offices duties	
	7/11		Commenced apparatus & observance School of Instruction. Training as to requirements.	
	8/11		Trades School and conferred until (ord) as to requirements. Normal duties	

Army Form C. 2118

WAR DIARY
or
INTELLIGENCE SUMMARY
(Erase heading not required.)

Instructions regarding War Diaries and Intelligence Summaries are contained in F. S. Regs., Part II. and the Staff Manual respectively. Title Pages will be prepared in manuscript.

Place	Date	Hour	Summary of Events and Information	Remarks and references to Appendices
LECAUROY				
	10/11		normal duties	
	11/11		normal duties	
	12/11		Began erection of workshop annex to carpenters shop of present ordnance shop. Fitted heavy mobile workshop with a view to obtain adaption for a gas cylinders of similar houses.	
	13/11		normal duties	
	14/11		normal duties	
	15/11		Question of fitting the area with Camps bath water, pumps hand fire. Oxygen stores. Gas iBene demanded from Base	

WAR DIARY
or
INTELLIGENCE SUMMARY

(Erase heading not required.)

Army Form C. 2118

Instructions regarding War Diaries and Intelligence Summaries are contained in F. S. Regs., Part II. and the Staff Manual respectively. Title Pages will be prepared in manuscript.

Place	Date	Hour	Summary of Events and Information	Remarks and references to Appendices
LECAUROY	16/11		O.C. Signal Co. regrets manufacture of Signal panels for aeroplane work. R.F.C. unable to land any check and panels made arrangements to obtain these.	
	17/11		Arrival of Boots F.S. in all cases well no smokers. F.O.O. states fr 1st Bn. 1st stores off and issued Base fr instructors.	
	18/11		Re arrangement of ammunition out Batt. An ammunition left out with each Bn. This brought out Bn. O.K.P. G.O.C. approves of promotion of S/Sgt. Brooke to act. W.O. without pay.	
	19/11		Normal work	

WAR DIARY
or
INTELLIGENCE SUMMARY
(Erase heading not required.)

Army Form C. 2118

Instructions regarding War Diaries and Intelligence Summaries are contained in F. S. Regs., Part II. and the Staff Manual respectively. Title Pages will be prepared in manuscript.

Place	Date	Hour	Summary of Events and Information	Remarks and references to Appendices
1st ARMY	20/11		Stamping of Lewis Drums Mark II - Progress	
	21/11		Arrival of S/S E. VETTS Army Act. Inspector of Machine & Lewis Guns - Complaint from unit that present manufacture of butt swell is not of the best workmanship	
	22/11		Lewis unit with S/S E. VETTS making Examination of Machine Guns	
	23/11		Visited units of 42nd Bde - Arrival of Small Arms Box Respirators	
	24/11		Normal duties	
	25/11		Visited units of 41st Bde	
	26/11		Continued Examination of Lewis Guns	

WAR DIARY or INTELLIGENCE SUMMARY

Army Form C. 2118

Place	Date	Hour	Summary of Events and Information	Remarks and references to Appendices
CAUROY	27/11		Sent instructions to bring all machine guns into shop for careful overhaul.	
	28/11		Normal duties.	
	29/11		Arrived VI Corps if inspection of Lt. EVETIS & 30 puffs Junior examination of Lewis Guns	
	30/11		Normal duties in Office	

CONFIDENTIAL

Vol 19

WAR DIARY

OF

D.A.D.O.S., 14th DIVISION

From 1-12-16 To 31-12-16

WAR DIARY or INTELLIGENCE SUMMARY

Army Form C. 2118

Place	Date	Hour	Summary of Events and Information	Remarks and references to Appendices
LECHUOY	1/12/16		Purchase material for manufacture of Signal panels. No spare panels to be made up for each unit pilots in reserve	
	2/12		Normal duties	
	3/12		Arrival of 9" and 10" Lewis Gun per batt. Careful examination made of those in Ammunition shop. Pioneer Batt. alive only to retain 8.	
	4/12		Normal duties.	
	5/12		Visit to 61 Trels Co. with A.D.V.S. Inspection of transport and armoury of outstanding indents.	
	6/12		Normal duties. 1st Div R.A. come into rest area. Rifle finishes	
	7/12		Issue of Bot Respirators begun to R.A. Visit returning old pattern Box Respirators. Examination being made of arul returns by Gas Officer	

WAR DIARY
or
INTELLIGENCE SUMMARY

(Erase heading not required.)

Army Form C. 2118

Place	Date	Hour	Summary of Events and Information	Remarks and references to Appendices
LE COWDRY	8/12/15		Sent request to O.C. Batts. to permit regular visits to Ordnance Dump for purpose of going into exhalatory questions & reviewing interests.	
"	9/12		Heavy hostile shops making 60 cradles for wheels of T.M. carts	
"	10/12		Visited S.A.S.O. 12 Div with view to Exchange dumps	
"	11/12		A draft of reinforcements arrived without proper equipment & Personal Kit. Also no blankets. Rewire position to Div. boots. Army Greatcoats 800 blankets. Shall report to Gen. Hqrs. as to condition of their men	
"	12/12		Normal duties	
"	13/12		Normal duties	
"	14/12		Normal duties	

Army Form C. 2118

WAR DIARY
or
INTELLIGENCE SUMMARY
(Erase heading not required.)

Instructions regarding War Diaries and Intelligence Summaries are contained in F. S. Regs., Part II. and the Staff Manual respectively. Title Pages will be prepared in manuscript.

Place	Date	Hour	Summary of Events and Information	Remarks and references to Appendices
LE CAUROY	15/12		Question of number of pack ponies allowed to Batt. areas suit 10" SB. 9. VI Corps rules 10 as per 9/098 but re the general case allows one set for M.O.	
	16/12		Home of 14" Bw units leave artillery command for 19" inst.	
	17/12		Reported that 111" RA to be left in rest area to VI Corps.	
	18/12		ADST instructs SADOS 12 Bn to administer above. Rept of 11" & 12" Seige Bns for Battn. 9" 11" & 12" Seige Bns. Gunners at VI Corps are stores transferred to MARCUS. Gunners at VI Corps are stores transferred to MARCUS.	
WARLUS	19/12		Offices opened at MARCUS. 12" Bn RA units transferred from 12 Bn SADOS. to 14 Bn SADOS.	
	20/12		Visits O.C. 14" Bn Depot Battn. & made list of necessary equipment. Forward in regard for authority thereof Div Hqrs. to Army.	

WAR DIARY
or
INTELLIGENCE SUMMARY

Army Form C. 2118

(Erase heading not required.)

Instructions regarding War Diaries and Intelligence Summaries are contained in F.S. Regs., Part II. and the Staff Manual respectively. Title Pages will be prepared in manuscript.

Place	Date	Hour	Summary of Events and Information	Remarks and references to Appendices
MARLES	21/12		Requests for Supcer blankets &c, received	
"	22/12		Conveyances despatches by 12 Bn. which went to take over.	
	22/12		Adjustment of hired alain & ammunition.	
	23/12		Loan of our stoves to Town keeper	
	24/12		Normal duties	
	25/12		Normal duties	
	26/12		Normal duties	
	27/12		Attachment of N.C.O. Special Bee N.C. for Ordnance Duties	
	28/12		Normal duties	
	29/12		Recie of units' indents	
	30/12		Normal duties	
	31/12		Normal duties	

h. Kenleys
D.A.D.O.S.
14th Div.

Jan 1917

Army Form C. 2118

DADOS

WAR DIARY
or
INTELLIGENCE SUMMARY
(Erase heading not required.)

Instructions regarding War Diaries and Intelligence Summaries are contained in F.S. Regs., Part II. and the Staff Manual respectively. Title Pages will be prepared in manuscript.

Place	Date	Hour	Summary of Events and Information	Remarks and references to Appendices
WARLUS	1/1/17		Normal duties.	
"	2/1		Normal duties.	
"	3/1		Arrival of new type Bomber Shells and Silk needles. The shells appear to be too heavy.	
"	4/1		Horse of Adjutant arrived for the day now cancelled. Purchase of horses in DOULLENS.	
"	5/1		Score of Pailhaes races & Town trap. Visit of D.D.V.S. Third Army. Visit of A.D.V.S. IV Corps	
"	6/1		Normal duties.	

WAR DIARY
or
INTELLIGENCE SUMMARY

Army Form C. 2118

Place	Date	Hour	Summary of Events and Information	Remarks and references to Appendices
WARLUS	7/1/17		Visited Skin Hosp. R.A. and learned that 14" R.A. would be transferred back to 14 Div. on 9" inst.	
	8/1		Visited A.D.M.S. 111 Corps.	
	9/1		Sthenia now transferred to 111 Corps from 17 Corps. 14" R.A. now transferred to 14 Div. 12" R.A. now transferred to 12 Div. Got receipts of Gun Books Kept.	
	10/1		Visited O/c Div. Train.	
	11/1		Normal duties.	
	12/1		Began a tour of 14" Div. Lines today.	

Army Form C. 2118

WAR DIARY
or
INTELLIGENCE SUMMARY
(Erase heading not required.)

Place	Date	Hour	Summary of Events and Information	Remarks and references to Appendices
WAMUS	13/4/17		Difficulty with Railhead. Arrival of kinds very uncertain. Railhead SAULTY.	
"	14/4/17		Visited section of D.A.C. unpacked vintage	
"	15/4/17		Continued visit of Town kays	
"	16/-		Visited A.D.T.T. VIII Corps	
"	17/-		Normal duties	
"	18/-		Conference of D.A.D.T.T. at VIII Corps	
"	19/-		Visited Railhead. Normal duties.	

Army Form C. 2118

WAR DIARY
or
INTELLIGENCE SUMMARY
(Erase heading not required.)

Instructions regarding War Diaries and Intelligence Summaries are contained in F.S. Regs., Part II. and the Staff Manual respectively. Title Pages will be prepared in manuscript.

Place	Date	Hour	Summary of Events and Information	Remarks and references to Appendices
MARLUS	20/-		Visited D.O.M. with reference 2" T.M. with mechanisms	
"	21/-		Normal duties	
"	22/-		Visited Heavy hostile howitzer. Arranged to have a supply of nicks made for Lewis Gun magazines	
"	23/-		Conducted visit to Town Major	
"	24/-		Normal duties	
"	25/-		Arrival of 13" & 14" Lewis Guns for Battn.	
"	26/-		New Lewis Gun magazines carefully overhauled & kept	
"	27/-		Truck at Rocher's arrived, had to send lorry etc as not available from Li not to heap to MUBILUX	

The line very unsettled.

WAR DIARY
or
INTELLIGENCE SUMMARY

Army Form C. 2118

Place	Date	Hour	Summary of Events and Information	Remarks and references to Appendices
MARLUS	27/1		Took S.O.T. Maw Act: Staff Capt. R.A. to 9.O.M. Went into diffculties experienced with 2" T.M.	
"	28/1		normal duties	
"	29/1		Local purchase of marking clerk for identity marks for outlins. Respect of return of labour employed to N.O.T. Corps.	
	30/1		Visit of A.D.O.S. VII Corps. Question of best method of administering of Artillery from guns now to another unit discussed.	
	31/1		Preparation of Loans report. Prepared Salvage return. Visit of B.A.D.O.S. 30 Div. 47 Bde R.F.A. withdrawn from the line.	

M. Healy/r
S.A.D.O.S.
1st Army

CONFIDENTIAL.

WAR DIARY

D.A.D.O.S. 14. DIV.

From February 1st 1917.
To February 28th 1917.

Army Form C. 2118

WAR DIARY
or
INTELLIGENCE SUMMARY
(Erase heading not required.)

Instructions regarding War Diaries and Intelligence Summaries are contained in F.S. Regs., Part II. and the Staff Manual respectively. Title Pages will be prepared in manuscript.

Place	Date	Hour	Summary of Events and Information	Remarks and references to Appendices
WARLUS	1/3/17		Normal duties in Mud + dump.	
	2/3		Notice given to releapt part of dump due to arrival & unloading of another Divisional dump. Between 15 cwts at rear of present dump.	
	3/3		Despatch of monthly issue return to VIII Corps. Figures much bigger than average. Reason supposed to be heavy use of clothing reinforcements, and also very heavy weather. Despatch of monthly receipt of Salvage to VIII Corps. Here figures continue to increase and it would appear that units are now returning more unserviceable stores in response to letters issued on the subject from time to time. Despatch of monthly return of boots repaired to VIII Corps. The return shows considerable improvement and would be much better if supplies of leather were not so short.	

WAR DIARY or INTELLIGENCE SUMMARY

Army Form C. 2118

(Erase heading not required.)

Instructions regarding War Diaries and Intelligence Summaries are contained in F.S. Regs., Part II. and the Staff Manual respectively. Title Pages will be prepared in manuscript.

Place	Date	Hour	Summary of Events and Information	Remarks and references to Appendices
WARLUS	4/2/17		Normal duties. Visit of A.D.V.S VII Corps.	
"	5/2/17		Local purchase made of twine and material for lantern chops, brushes & dubbin for O.C. VII Corps machine pack for 14 R.E. and statement for 14 R.E.	
"	6/2/17		Individuals to further allotment of Vizors. Also of Body shields & neckets. One 3" Stokes mortar received from 118 Bde T.M.B. Report of c/vonalty car to Hqrs to Third Army. Paid a visit to 91 Inf Bde & gave them the slaves	
"	7/2/17		to 118 Bde Hq. Reports that post cars were guided to Gave instructions to demand further supply and forwarded to that a reserve Violets & impants Shoemakers Armourer also Repr Bath.	
"	8/2/17		Took over duties of Salvage Officer during leave of that officer.	

Army Form C. 2118

WAR DIARY
or
INTELLIGENCE SUMMARY
(Erase heading not required.)

Instructions regarding War Diaries and Intelligence Summaries are contained in F. S. Regs., Part II. and the Staff Manual respectively. Title Pages will be prepared in manuscript.

Place	Date	Hour	Summary of Events and Information	Remarks and references to Appendices
WARLUS	9/2/17		Normal duties	
"	10/2		Foot inspection and units demanding great care and great pains, decide to hold a small course in future during winter months.	
"	11/2		Inspected shops at Depot Battn. Found many men being sent to courses with bulged barrels rifles. The bootmakers shop proving very useful.	
"	12/2		Normal duties	
"	13/2		Normal duties	
"	14/2		Inspection of Lewis Guns at School of Instruction. one surplus to be handed over to 9th Div.	
"	15/2		D.D.T.S. Third Army visited the dumps. Expressed satisfaction. Promised to sanction further issue of two more Lewis guns to each Batt.	

WAR DIARY or INTELLIGENCE SUMMARY

Army Form C. 2118

(Erase heading not required.)

Instructions regarding War Diaries and Intelligence Summaries are contained in F.S. Regs., Part II. and the Staff Manual respectively. Title Pages will be prepared in manuscript.

Place	Date	Hour	Summary of Events and Information	Remarks and references to Appendices
WARLUS	16/2		Normal duties	
"	17/2		Limits asking for further issue of gum boots thigh. All issues from Army to Division have to large proportion of useless sizes. Average sizes $6^s, 7^s, 8^s, \& 9^s$. Gas precautions announced.	
"	18/2		Normal duties	
"	19/2		Inspected area, also at Iron harness dump. Found village in bad condition.	
"	20/2		Great difficulty experienced by loss of lorry transport due to Gas precautions. Railhead complained at loss of time due to horse transport not draw'g promptly.	
"	21/2		Established a dump at SAULTY village as horse transport not equal to task of bring'g stores from SAULTY railhead to WARLUS.	

1875 Wt. W593/826 1,000,000 4/15 J.B.C. & A. A.D.S.S./Forms/C. 2118.

Army Form C. 2118

WAR DIARY
or
INTELLIGENCE SUMMARY
(Erase heading not required.)

Place	Date	Hour	Summary of Events and Information	Remarks and references to Appendices
WARLUS	22/2		All rooms suspended at WARLUS dump. Lorries begun at SAULTY dump. Special passes granted to certain ranks by APM to draw special stores. One man sent to Base with Sturt Stewart Slipper machine heads by special arrangement with GOC Base. Man to bring back shaped blades. Work continuing at tent dump.	
"	23/2		Two Stokes J. mortars kunst. Mortars sent to J OM.	
"	24/2		Am to Base for special inspection.	
"	25/2		Wanted B.T.O 42 Bos. a gallon of transport of Natives, khaki and ammunition on pack animals. Inspected specially filled pack arrival for transport.	
"	26/2		Six 2 gall. petrol tins filled with water. Normal duties	

Army Form C. 2118

WAR DIARY
or
INTELLIGENCE SUMMARY
(Erase heading not required.)

Instructions regarding War Diaries and Intelligence Summaries are contained in F. S. Regs., Part II. and the Staff Manual respectively. Title Pages will be prepared in manuscript.

Place	Date	Hour	Summary of Events and Information	Remarks and references to Appendices
WARLUS	27/2		Arrived 8 Bn from 9.45 7 M.S. for 1/14 7 M Bg. Their trip brought us in turned by night.	
	28/2		Normal duties. Preparation of qunnly relieve	

M. Cole Col.
L.M D.T.T
1st Bn.

1875 Wt. W593/826 1,000,000 4/15 J.B.C. & A. A.D.S.S./Forms/C. 2118.

Confidential   No. 2

WAR DIARY

D.A.D.O.S.
+ Div.

From Mar 1st - 1917
To Mar 31st 1917

W. Henderson
DADOS
14 Div.

Army Form C. 2118

WAR DIARY
or
INTELLIGENCE SUMMARY
(Erase heading not required.)

Instructions regarding War Diaries and Intelligence Summaries are contained in F. S. Regs., Part II. and the Staff Manual respectively. Title Pages will be prepared in manuscript.

Place	Date	Hour	Summary of Events and Information	Remarks and references to Appendices
WARLUS	1/3/17		Preparation of monthly returns due to this Army.	
	2/3/17		Normal duties.	
	3/3/17		Dispatch of monthly returns to III Corps. Notes that clothing demands still high and this thought to be due to very bad weather. Return of boots repaired in the Division shews a decrease, but this is due to Base curtailing supplies of grindery.	
	4/3/17		B.A.D.O.S. granted leave from 5th - 14th inst.	
	5/3/17		Normal duties in office and dump.	
	6/3/17		Normal duties.	

1875 Wt. W593/826 1,000,000 4/15 J.B.C. & A. A.D.S.S./Forms/C. 2118.

Army Form C. 2118

WAR DIARY
or
INTELLIGENCE SUMMARY
(Erase heading not required.)

Instructions regarding War Diaries and Intelligence Summaries are contained in F.S. Regs., Part II. and the Staff Manual respectively. Title Pages will be prepared in manuscript.

Place	Date	Hour	Summary of Events and Information	Remarks and references to Appendices
MARLES	7/3/17		Tailors began manufacture of special armlets for infantry runners, bombers etc.	
"	8/3/17		Snow affected MT transport. Cobs were not allowed loaded on G.S. wagons for Oldinin stores — due to thaw precautions.	
	9/3/17		Base asking if frost nails may be withdrawn now. A.D.V.S. Sur and A.D.V.S. VIII Corps both of matter replied to A.D.V.S. that this should not be done for at least a week when agree that the "whim agree that..." Division receiving one Auto Steward Grinder from Base on allotment. This handed to O.C. Mobile Vet. Section.	
	10/3/17			
	11/3/17		Issue of 6 cu Ration Right being made to units. Three being fixed in Ambulance Obsp.	

Army Form C. 2118

WAR DIARY
or
INTELLIGENCE SUMMARY
(Erase heading not required.)

Instructions regarding War Diaries and Intelligence Summaries are contained in F.S. Regs., Part II. and the Staff Manual respectively. Title Pages will be prepared in manuscript.

Place	Date	Hour	Summary of Events and Information	Remarks and references to Appendices
WARLUS	12-3-17		Normal duties.	
"	13-		Normal duties.	
"	14		D.A.D.V.S. returned from leave.	
"	15.		Visited Railhead and arranged to dump stores owing to difficulty of transport due to bad roads.	
"	16.		Stopped departure of stores from Base 'due to lack of transport on roads.	
"	17		Normal duties.	
"	18		Opened allotment of pack artillery mains termis for carriage of rations and water on pack animals.	
"	19.		Normal duties	

Army Form C. 2118

WAR DIARY
or
INTELLIGENCE SUMMARY
(Erase heading not required.)

Instructions regarding War Diaries and Intelligence Summaries are contained in F. S. Regs., Part II. and the Staff Manual respectively. Title Pages will be prepared in manuscript. 1917

Place	Date	Hour	Summary of Events and Information	Remarks and references to Appendices
WARLUS	20/3		Issue of Sponge Goggles to scale of one per man throughout the Bde.	
	21/3		Notice of attachment of 40th Army Troops Artillery from 21st Bde to 1st Div.	
	22/3		Normal duties.	
	23/3		Attached 232nd Army Troops Artillery B.A.C. for Ordnance administration.	
	24/3		Visited School of Instruction with S.A. + M.G. Sec. Decided R.E. Armourer and Bootmaker should remain with School on its transfer to 1st Corps as a temporary measure.	
	25/3		Normal duties.	
	26/3		Began fitting of special rifle attachments to "9.45" Trench Mortars.	

1875 Wt. W593/826 1,000,000 4/15 J.B.C. & A. A.D.S.S./Forms/C. 2118.

WAR DIARY or INTELLIGENCE SUMMARY

Army Form C. 2118

Instructions regarding War Diaries and Intelligence Summaries are contained in F.S. Regs., Part II. and the Staff Manual respectively. Title Pages will be prepared in manuscript.

(Erase heading not required.)

Place	Date	Hour	Summary of Events and Information	Remarks and references to Appendices
WARLUS	27/3		Issue of Sponge Anti-Gas Goggles begun on scale of one per man throughout the Division.	
"	28/3		Visited 3rd Army Trench Mortar School and secured accurate Clinometers in exchange for old instruments.	
"	29/3		Visit of D.D.V.S. 3rd Army + A.D.V.S. VII Corps	
"	29/3		Conference at VII Corps for B.A.D.V.S. + A.D.V.S.	
"	30/3		232 A.A. artillery report shortage of one 18 p.r. gun. Wired A.D.V.S. 46 for particulars.	
"	31/3		46 too unable to give information as to probable date. Wired Base. Base replied had gun up on 241.	

Reported to R.O.D. VIII Corps for G. action.

h. Heath ½
L.A.V.T. - 14 Div
2.3.17

Vol 23

WAR DIARY.

DADOS
14 DIV

APRIL 1st – 30th – 1917

CONFIDENTIAL

M. Keate (?)
DADOS
14th Div.

Army Form C. 2118

WAR DIARY
or
INTELLIGENCE SUMMARY
(Erase heading not required.)

Instructions regarding War Diaries and Intelligence Summaries are contained in F.S. Regs., Part II. and the Staff Manual respectively. Title Pages will be prepared in manuscript.

Place	Date	Hour	Summary of Events and Information	Remarks and references to Appendices
NARLUS	1/4		Special preparations in progress for active operations. Move of 41" by Bde n/h reserve area. 42" & 43" Bdes into the line.	
	2/4		Warning operation order received. Normal routine	
	3/4		Arrival of Lt. J.W.A. BURBIDGE, A.O.C. for instruction and report.	
	4/4		New rackhead at GOUY.	
	5/4		Completion of Air-exp't check for Signal Co. Received instructions from Hgr. Div. that dump must be at GOUY.	

WAR DIARY or INTELLIGENCE SUMMARY

Army Form C. 2118

Place	Date	Hour	Summary of Events and Information	Remarks and references to Appendices
MARUS	6/4		Inspected Divisional Ammunition Dumps	
	7/4		Visits two 1st Line Workshops	
	8/4		Inspection of transport camp at BERNEVILLE	
	9/4		Normal issues and repairs pending operations	
	9/4		Operations commenced. Ammunition dump at GOUY opened.	
			Visited Ordnance Gun Park at PREVENT.	
	10/4		Normal duties	
	11/4		Units being withdrawn from the line.	
			Preparations being made for re-equipping units. GOUY dump closed.	

Army Form C. 2118

WAR DIARY
or
INTELLIGENCE SUMMARY
(Erase heading not required.)

Instructions regarding War Diaries and Intelligence Summaries are contained in F.S. Regs., Part II. and the Staff Manual respectively. Title Pages will be prepared in manuscript.

Place	Date	Hour	Summary of Events and Information	Remarks and references to Appendices
WARLUS	12/4		Units moving to LE CAUROY area. R.A. remaining in the line until 5.0.p.m.	
"	13/4		Normal duties	
"	14/4		Normal duties	
"	15/4		Tour of units and interviews with C.O.'s and Quartermasters on shortages and losses. Bulk are sent to Base for special battle equipment stores.	
"	16/4		Informed by Hqrs. Division that units were probably returning to the line about 18" and must be quickly refitted.	
"	17/4		Established dump at LE CAUROY. Retained stores of various sorts until 23rd inst.	
"	18/4		Orders not to move into line until 25th inst.	
"	19/4		Refitting of units continuing.	

WAR DIARY
or
INTELLIGENCE SUMMARY

(Erase heading not required.)

Army Form C. 2118

Place	Date	Hour	Summary of Events and Information	Remarks and references to Appendices
WARLUS	20/4		Normal duties	
"	21/4		Salving of Lewis Gun magazines, hand buckets and equipment for re-issue.	
"	22/4		Arrangements completed for baths and charge of underclothing. FWD baths working well. Allotment of stores for the purpose.	
"	23/4		Hqrs moved to BAILLEUMONT. Temporary dump closed at LE CAUROY.	
"	24/4		Units moving up nearer the line. Reported to Hqrs Div as Lt J.N.A BURBIDGE	
"	25/4		Hqrs moved into ARRAS and take over from 50 Div.	
"	26/4		Took over Ordnance dump at 13, Rue de L'Abbé Halluin. ARRAS from ARDOS 50 Div. Also administration of 50" R.A.	

WAR DIARY
or
INTELLIGENCE SUMMARY

(Erase heading not required.)

Army Form C. 2118

Place	Date	Hour	Summary of Events and Information	Remarks and references to Appendices
ARRAS	27/4		Part of shops moved into dump at ARRAS. Other part retained at WARLUS.	
	28/4		normal work	
	29/4		Salvage Co. arrangements completed. Dump to be near NEUVILLE VITASSE.	
	30/4		Blowing up of ruin villages of van Oloi and solvage begun by units during march forward into line. Bearing operation orders received in reference to offensive to take place about May 3rd.	

h. Headley
D.A.D.T.
1st Div

14
Appx 24

WAR DIARY

May 1st to
May 31st 1917

DADOS 14 Div

CONFIDENTIAL

Army Form C. 2118

WAR DIARY
or
INTELLIGENCE SUMMARY
(Erase heading not required.)

Instructions regarding War Diaries and Intelligence Summaries are contained in F. S. Regs., Part II. and the Staff Manual respectively. Title Pages will be prepared in manuscript.

Place	Date	Hour	Summary of Events and Information	Remarks and references to Appendices
ARRAS	1/5		Normal duties.	
"	2/5		Units starting to. Very few stores being taken.	
"	3/5		Preparation of monthly returns for books.	
"	4/5		Normal duties	
"	5/5		Great loss of Lewis magazines. Salvage Co. obtaining as many as possible over their being cleaned and repaired and received	
"	6/5		Corps asking for record of arrival of trucks from Base.	
"	7/5		Normal duties.	
"	8/5		Units reporting serious loss of Lewis Guns / Keep check fire / casualties. Think one Lewis Guns + his Vickers lost by Division during offensive action.	

1875 Wt. W593/826 1,000,000 4/15 J.B.C. & A. A.D.S.S./Forms/C. 2118.

Army Form C. 2118

WAR DIARY
or
INTELLIGENCE SUMMARY
(Erase heading not required.)

Instructions regarding War Diaries and Intelligence Summaries are contained in F. S. Regs., Part II. and the Staff Manual respectively. Title Pages will be prepared in manuscript.

Place	Date	Hour	Summary of Events and Information	Remarks and references to Appendices
ARRAS	9/5		A.D.O.S. in to advise that Observer dump be moved out of ARRAS.	
	10/5		Selected new site on BEAURAINS-MERCATEL road and reported proposed move.	
	11/5		Moved stores from ARRAS to new site. Also moved stores from WANCUS 1/6 AGNY to Retaining Stores at ARRAS further move of burden at 14½ central about 57c.	
	12/5		Dump and Stores now at M.17.c central about 57c.	
	13/5		Visited Salvage dump and gave directions as to disposal of received stores.	
	14/5		Normal duties.	
	15/5		Large number of Lewis Gun magazines being salved (cleaned & rewound).	

WAR DIARY
or
INTELLIGENCE SUMMARY

(Erase heading not required.)

Army Form C. 2118

Place	Date	Hour	Summary of Events and Information	Remarks and references to Appendices
M.17 c central Sheet 57c	16/5/17		Conference of D.A.D'O.S at VII. Corps.	
	17/5		Visited transport lines of "42" Inf Bde incl B & D Coy Bn inspecting kitbags.	
			Shops engaged in Salvaging & repairing rifles.	
			Large numbers required due to increased establishment for P.S.A. Btys.	
	18/5		Normal duties	
	19/5		Normal duties	
	20/5		Requested an allotment of chaff-cutters to transport lines of VII Corps	
	21/5		Second visit for a more complete return of clothing released by scheme of new.	

Army Form C. 2118

WAR DIARY
or
INTELLIGENCE SUMMARY
(Erase heading not required.)

Place	Date	Hour	Summary of Events and Information	Remarks and references to Appendices
M17c central	22/5/17		Normal duties	
"	23/5		Requested an allotment of kits from VII. Corps	
	24/5		Visit of A.D.D.S Third Army.	
	25/5		Visit of ADOS VII Corps who received orders.	
	26/5		VII Corps promise 9 days clothes and 199 kits as seen above	
	27/5		Normal duties	
	28/5		Issue of 200 rifles made from Ordnance workshop 1st Corps.	
	29/5		Departure of Lt. J. Burbidge A.O.C. (2 Lieut. duty) at SB Ord.	
	30/5 – 5/5		Normal duties. Preparation of monthly returns.	W. Henley

CONFIDENTIAL.

WAR DIARY

DADOS
14 DIV.

June 1st – June 30th
1917.

M. Heale[?]
DADOS
14 Div.

Army Form C. 2118

WAR DIARY
or
INTELLIGENCE SUMMARY
(Erase heading not required.)

Instructions regarding War Diaries and Intelligence Summaries are contained in F. S. Regs., Part II. and the Staff Manual respectively. Title Pages will be prepared in manuscript.

Place	Date	Hour	Summary of Events and Information	Remarks and references to Appendices
M.17 c.	1/6/17		Preparation of monthly returns	
	2/6/17		Visit of A.D.V.S. In Corps Inspector's horse Vet Section	
	3/6/17		Visited 4th Co. Sup. Train	
	4/6/17		Normal duties. Arrival of Lt. FIELD to inspect Leave Pass.	
	5/6/17		Normal duties	
	6/6/17		Normal duties	
	7/6/17		Preparation for move of unit of area.	

WAR DIARY
or
INTELLIGENCE SUMMARY

(Erase heading not required.)

Army Form C. 2118

Place	Date	Hour	Summary of Events and Information	Remarks and references to Appendices
M.I.R.C Central Sheet 51 c	8/6/17		Difficulty experienced in procuring centres paid from Base. Base still quite unable to provide regular Guardsmen. Obtained two thousand from front line.	
	9/6/17		Till but regret reason for the large increase in demand for population. Explanation is apparently "because of January". Garments sent up – most of them being second hand washes.	
	10/6/17		Inspected Lewis Guns of 9", KRRC and 9 KRB with L. 2nd Graphite of Lewis Guns. Found them in very good order.	
MARIEUX	11/6/17		Moved to MARIEUX. All went two Artillery, Lc & Co Train in motors. Heavy dust made Bys.	
	12/6/17		Inspection of Lewis Guns continued.	

WAR DIARY or INTELLIGENCE SUMMARY

Army Form C. 2118

(Erase heading not required.)

Place	Date	Hour	Summary of Events and Information	Remarks and references to Appendices
MARIEUX	13/6/17		Re-equipment of Bn. units commenced	
	14/6/17		Visited town Major in town with view to making provision of washing head & baths in the village	
	15/6/17		Sent out armourers & one Batt. to overhaul rifles & Lewis Guns.	
	16/6/17		7 Coys to Lewis Gun School and took Lewis Guns on Divi. stage.	
	17/6/17		Transferred Capt. T Harrison A.O.C from us Batt. to VIII Corps Reserve.	
	18/6/17		Difficulty experienced in obtaining shops to repair of vehicles	
	19/6/17		Instructed units through "D.R.O" to make up all deficiencies i.e. equipment.	

Army Form C. 2118

WAR DIARY
or
INTELLIGENCE SUMMARY
(Erase heading not required.)

Place	Date	Hour	Summary of Events and Information	Remarks and references to Appendices
WARIEUX	21/6/17		Transfer of Guild Cos. & Pioneers bulks. to this Army for action due to New units move to Second Army	
	22/6/17			
	23/6/17		Completion of conversion of Lewis Guns & rifles by L. Field. A.O.D.	
	24/6/17		normal duties	
	25/6/17		Transfer of L. Guns A.O.D. to 50" Divn.	
	26/6/17		A.D.S.S. proceeds on leave	
	27/6/17		normal duties	
	28/6/17			

Army Form C. 2118

WAR DIARY
or
INTELLIGENCE SUMMARY
(Erase heading not required.)

Instructions regarding War Diaries and Intelligence Summaries are contained in F. S. Regs., Part II. and the Staff Manual respectively. Title Pages will be prepared in manuscript.

Place	Date	Hour	Summary of Events and Information	Remarks and references to Appendices
MARIEUX	29/6		Vehicles for repair being taken to FTT bank workshop at NEUVILLE VITASSE	
"	29/6		Lorries order issued for move of Coy to Lucaux Army.	
	30/6		Normal duties.	

M. Heab Capt.
D.A.D.S.T.
1st Army

Vol 26

CONFIDENTIAL.

WAR DIARY

JULY 1st 1917
to
JULY 31st 1917

DADOS. 14 DIV.

Army Form C. 2118

WAR DIARY
or
INTELLIGENCE SUMMARY
(Erase heading not required.)

Instructions regarding War Diaries and Intelligence Summaries are contained in F. S. Regs., Part II. and the Staff Manual respectively. Title Pages will be prepared in manuscript.

Place	Date	Hour	Summary of Events and Information	Remarks and references to Appendices
MARŒUIL	1/7		Normal duties. Division two 17 Pioneers & R.E. 6o's rest.	
"	2/7		Normal duties	
"	3/7		Normal duties	
"	4/7		Horses being overhauled at NEUVILLE VITASSE	
"	5/7		S.A.D.O.S. returned from leave	
"	6/7		Preparations for move	
"	7/7		Normal duties	
"	8/7		Normal duties	
"	9/7		Visited S. JANS CAPPEL and selected a site	

Army Form C. 2118

WAR DIARY
or
INTELLIGENCE SUMMARY
(Erase heading not required.)

Instructions regarding War Diaries and Intelligence Summaries are contained in F.S. Regs., Part II. and the Staff Manual respectively. Title Pages will be prepared in manuscript.

Place	Date	Hour	Summary of Events and Information	Remarks and references to Appendices
MARIEUX	10/7		Units moving.	
"	11/7		Moved Ordnance Dump to S. JANS. CAPPEL	
"	12/7		Units on the move	
S. JANS. CAPPEL	13/7		Reported to A.D.O.S IX Corps	
"	14/7		Reported general condition of equipment of units to D.D.O.S Second Army.	
"	15/7		Visited heavy howitzer workshops	
"	16/7		14" R.A. units transferred from 39th Div. to 1st Div. for administration	
"	17/7		Visited S.O.M. at IX. Corps.	
"	18/7		View of D.D.O.S Second Army	
"	19/7		Reported difficulty in getting new guns to replace casualties. Shops erected in Dump. Armourer tailor begun work again	

Army Form C. 2118

WAR DIARY
or
INTELLIGENCE SUMMARY
(Erase heading not required.)

Instructions regarding War Diaries and Intelligence Summaries are contained in F. S. Regs., Part II. and the Staff Manual respectively. Title Pages will be prepared in manuscript.

Place	Date	Hour	Summary of Events and Information	Remarks and references to Appendices
S-JANS CAPPEL	20/7		Normal duties	
"	21/7		Shortage of Pine Bush Stock for Lewis Guns. This is a serious weakness in the Lewis Gun	
"	22/7		Posting of 249 machine Gun Co. to established of 1st Bn. Unit reports parts out from home & fitted will necessary.	
"	23/7		Visited depot. Battn. workshops, inspected Armourers, Bootmaker.	
"	24/7		Normal duties	
"	25/7		Overhaul of all bicycles of Battalions and Independent.	

1875 Wt. W593/826 1,000,000 4/15 J.B.C. & A. A.D.S.S./Forms/C. 2118.

Army Form C. 2118

Instructions regarding War Diaries and Intelligence Summaries are contained in F. S. Regs., Part II. and the Staff Manual respectively. Title Pages will be prepared in manuscript.

WAR DIARY
or
INTELLIGENCE SUMMARY
(Erase heading not required.)

Place	Date	Hour	Summary of Events and Information	Remarks and references to Appendices
S. JANS CAPPEL	26/7		Equipped Bath with full scale of summer underclothing	
	27/7		G.O.C. enquires into use of muzzle protectors. Tunic pattern unspecified. Scouts to equip all mounts with No 3. Mark 7 pattern.	
	28/7		Pulling of Vickers had IV mounts with depression stops	
	29/7		Normal duties	
	30/7		Issue of pack saddlery, crocks & walk him to work	
	31/7		Having order round to prepare to take over from 19" Bn.	

Vol 27

WAR DIARY.

D.A.D.O.S. 14 DIV.

Aug 1st — Aug 31st
1917.

M. Henderson
D.A.D.O.S.
14 Div.

CONFIDENTIAL

WAR DIARY
or
INTELLIGENCE SUMMARY

(Erase heading not required.)

Army Form C. 2118

Place	Date	Hour	Summary of Events and Information	Remarks and references to Appendices
1/8/17 – 31/8/17				
S. JAN. CAPPEL	1/8		Normal duties.	
"	2/8		Normal duties.	
"	3/8		Visited cooks of 41 Inf Bde.	
	4/8		G.O.C. requests that rifles be fitted with Mark III protectors. Very limited quantity at Base.	
	5/8		Issue of serum pair of cotton drawers to battle.	
	6/8		Division moves from S.JAN CAPPEL to CAESTRE	
	7/8		Transferred 14" R.A. to 36" Div. DADOS	

WAR DIARY or INTELLIGENCE SUMMARY

Army Form C. 2118

Place	Date	Hour	Summary of Events and Information	Remarks and references to Appendices
CAESTRE	8/6		Transferred 11th Corps Reinforcement Regt. to 24th Div.	
"	9/6		Normal duties	
"	10/6		Receipt of one hundred and fifty crates for carrying water tins from Decan Army Workshop	
"	11/6		Receipt of sixteen hundred water tins from Base	
"	12/6		Normal duties	
"	13/6		Departure of one W.O. and clerk to assist D.A.D.O.S 51st Div. with re "PA"	
"	14/6		Preparation for move from CAESTRE	

WAR DIARY or INTELLIGENCE SUMMARY

Army Form C. 2118

Place	Date	Hour	Summary of Events and Information	Remarks and references to Appendices
~~ST ANN CAPPEL~~				
CAESTRE	15/8		Reported to A.D.S. II Corps.	
	16/8		Moved with Div. to RENINGHELST. Took over 1st Div. R.A.	
RENINGHELST	17/8		1st Aust. Div. R.A. attached for administration from 1st Div.	
	18/8		Hqrs. Div. moved to advanced position ordnance dump retained at RENINGHELST.	
"	19/8		Visited Gun Park	
"	20/8		Visited 9.0.M.s 2nd " 22 & 55 workshops.	
	21/8		Enquiry being made into Ax Reciprocation for 18.P.R. Guns.	
	22/8		Issue of new horse ammunition to D.A.C.	

WAR DIARY or INTELLIGENCE SUMMARY

Army Form C. 2118

Place	Date	Hour	Summary of Events and Information	Remarks and references to Appendices
RENINGHELST	23/8		Visited units	
"	24/8		Visit of A.D.S.S. II Corps	
	25/8		Normal duties	
	26/8		Normal duties	
	27/8		Preparations for leaving area	
	28/8		Normal duties	
	29/8		Handing over Vet. stores to 23rd Div.	
	29/8		Div. moved to BERTHEN	
	30/8		Re-equipment of units	
	31/8		Preparations for move	

Vol 28

CONFIDENTIAL

WAR DIARY

Sept. 1st 1917
to
Sept 30 1917.

D.A.D.O.S
14 Division

M. Keele (?)
D.A.D.T.S
14 Div

Army Form C. 2118

WAR DIARY
or
INTELLIGENCE SUMMARY
(Erase heading not required.)

Instructions regarding War Diaries and Intelligence Summaries are contained in F. S. Regs., Part II. and the Staff Manual respectively. Title Pages will be prepared in manuscript.

Place	Date	Hour	Summary of Events and Information	Remarks and references to Appendices
BERTHEN	1/9		Moved to RAVELSBERG CAMP 28.S.1762.2	
	2/9		D.A.D.O.S office and dump placed at NEUVE EGLISE	
N. EGLISE	3/9		Normal duties.	
"	4/9		Visited 14th Div Depot Bath and inspected equipment of men arriving from Base	
"	5/9		Area Commandant appointed. Held consultation re methods of supply of Area stores	
"	6/9		Application made to Army for new fittings such as hook, check, lamps and brushes	
	7/9		Visited Second Army Heavy Mobile Workshops. Arrangements made to take over Cylinders for Stunbos Horns	

Army Form C. 2118

WAR DIARY
or
INTELLIGENCE SUMMARY

(Erase heading not required.)

Instructions regarding War Diaries and Intelligence Summaries are contained in F. S. Regs., Part II. and the Staff Manual respectively. Title Pages will be prepared in manuscript.

Place	Date	Hour	Summary of Events and Information	Remarks and references to Appendices
N. Leuze	8/9/17		Visited No 23 Light Mobile Workshop	
			Arrangements made to take Trench Mortars and R.A. instruments	
	9/9/17		Visited No 30 Light Mobile Workshop	
			Arrangements made to take all vehicles	
	10/9		Salvage dump established at side of Ordnance dump	
	11/9		Notice received from Div. HQrs that the dump would be re-opened	
	12/9		New dump established at 28.S.17.c.3.3. near Div. HQrs	
	13/9		Preparations made for move	
	14/9		Moved to new site	
	15/9		Normal duties	

WAR DIARY
or
INTELLIGENCE SUMMARY
(Erase heading not required.)

Army Form C. 2118

3

Place	Date	Hour	Summary of Events and Information	Remarks and references to Appendices
	16/9		Application for an allotment of gun boots made to Corps	
	17/9		Consideration given if Lewis Gun spare part bags. Experience of Bde units to be that complete bag filled with kit is the line, and that only a low percentage are brought back. Have a series of experiments with no bath and made a special bag to contain shop and contain his kit with a suggested list of spare parts to be carried in it.	
	18/9		Considerable difficulty experienced in having our O.T 18 P.R with the various workshops for repair of his leaving II Corps 24th Army. Found Res guns in charge of all Bde units were repaired and issued to units in other divisions. Visited Second Army and reported this.	
	19/9		Re arrangement of method of issue and use of Stein & Cappey machine. These machines no longer to be on unit charge, but held at a Divisional Clothing dump by the B.A.D.V.S.	

WAR DIARY
or
INTELLIGENCE SUMMARY
(Erase heading not required.)

Army Form C. 2118

Place	Date	Hour	Summary of Events and Information	Remarks and references to Appendices
	20/9		Issue of the first blankets per man to units proceeding up.	
	21/9		Experimenting with a special cover for Lewis Gun consisting of canvas cover for the radiator casing, laced on; also a canvas cover for the magazine and steel fasteners by quick release studs. Number being made for 449 Sqn. Bde. experiments.	
	22/9		Normal duties	
	23/9		Normal duties	
	24/9		Distribution of tables and forms to Area Camps	
	25/9		Re-equipment of 1st R.F.A. in progress. Shortage of Front Sights and carriers.	

Army Form C. 2118

WAR DIARY
or
INTELLIGENCE SUMMARY
(Erase heading not required.)

Instructions regarding War Diaries and Intelligence Summaries are contained in F. S. Regs., Part II. and the Staff Manual respectively. Title Pages will be prepared in manuscript.

Place	Date	Hour	Summary of Events and Information	Remarks and references to Appendices
	26/9		Considerable shortage in numbers reported to Second Army. An allotment promised.	
	27/9		Transfer of 249 M.G. Co. under orders to leave Division. Took items of equipment from 43 M.G. Co. to complete 249 M.G. Co.	
	28/9		Issue of winter underclothing proceeding from Base. Propose to hold winter clothing until winter conditions prevail.	
	29/9		Leave in chiefs to visits to overhaul boots & provision and animals to replace deficiencies.	
	30/9		Preparation of Quarterly returns due to Army Corps.	

h. Ledger.

1875 Wt. W593/826 1,000,000 4/15 J.B.C. & A. A.D.S.S./Forms/C. 2118.

CONFIDENTIAL

Vol 29

WAR DIARY

D.A.D.O.S. 14 DIV.

Oct 1st – Oct 31st 1917

WAR DIARY
or
INTELLIGENCE SUMMARY

(Erase heading not required.)

Army Form C. 2118

Place	Date	Hour	Summary of Events and Information	Remarks and references to Appendices
RAVELSBERG	1/4/17		Inspected Salvage Co. dump. Visited VIII Corps Salvage dump.	
"	2/4/17		Normal routine	
"	3/4/17		Subject of large dumps for events now taken up with Div. Q.	
"	4/4/17		Weather stormy. Part issue of underclothing made. Bath.	
"	5/4/17		Notice of proposed move given. All wires & arrangements cancelled.	
"	6/4/17		Been on the move.	

WAR DIARY or INTELLIGENCE SUMMARY

Army Form C. 2118

Place	Date	Hour	Summary of Events and Information	Remarks and references to Appendices
7-10-17	8/10/17		Moves from RAVELSBERG to WESTOUTRE. Normal duties	
WESTOUTRE	9/10/17		Transferred 14th R.A. to No. 33 D.iv. Normal duties	
	10/10/17		Normal duties	
	11		Left WESTOUTRE for LA CLYTE.	
LA CLYTE	12		Took over battle stores from ordnance 21st Div. and stored these in SCOTTISH WOOD	
"	13		Units unable to accept stores due to frequent moves and lack of storage in the forward area.	
"	14		Took over 33rd R.A. from Ord 7th Div.	
"	15		Demanded winter clothing for units. A.A. D.M.S. decided to refuse second blanket per man while in forward area.	

Army Form C. 2118

WAR DIARY
or
INTELLIGENCE SUMMARY
(Erase heading not required.)

Instructions regarding War Diaries and Intelligence Summaries are contained in F. S. Regs., Part II. and the Staff Manual respectively. Title Pages will be prepared in manuscript.

3

Place	Date	Hour	Summary of Events and Information	Remarks and references to Appendices
LA CLYTE	16/10		Normal duties.	
"	17/10		Normal duties	
"	18/10		Staff Sergt. 33rd R.A. reports that the units not I Foremen of any blankets or horse rugs. Arrangements being made to supply horse rugs to 33rd R.A. on loan from 33rd Division reserve.	
"	19/10		Horse gyps and clipping machines not carried to units of 1st Division desire. Several clipping'clothers key used under instructions of Senior army, when all clipping will be done and rugs issued.	
"	20/10			
"	21/10		Normal duties	

1875 Wt. W593/826 1,000,000 4/15 J.B.C. & A. A.D.S.S./Forms/C. 2118.

WAR DIARY
or
INTELLIGENCE SUMMARY

Army Form C. 2118

(Erase heading not required.)

Place	Date	Hour	Summary of Events and Information	Remarks and references to Appendices
LA CLYTTE	22/10		Visited units of 33rd R.A.; also Staff Sergt. 33rd R.A.	
	23/10		Visited 1st Div Quartermasters at transport lines in RIDGE WOOD.	
	24/10		Group moved to BERTHEN. Forward dump retained at LA CLYTTE to provide for three R.E. Cos. being retained in forward battle Infantry and three area for labour duties.	
BERTHEN	25/10		Transferred 33rd R.A. to advance 21st Division.	
	26/10		G.S. Staff transferred from or. 23 to O.). 1st Div. for special equipping & preparation for departure to another front.	

Army Form C. 2118

WAR DIARY
or
INTELLIGENCE SUMMARY
(Erase heading not required.)

Place	Date	Hour	Summary of Events and Information	Remarks and references to Appendices
BERTHEN	27/10		Completion of issue of second blanket, gloves, underwear & jackets to units of 1st Div.	
"	28/10		Horse Clippers found to be easily damaged when sent at Clipping Stations. Extra parts obtained from Base.	
"	29/10		Normal duties	
"	30/10		Normal duties. Preparation of monthly returns.	
"	31/10		Warning order received to prepare for move back ul next area	

M. Herald
D.A.D.V.S. 1st Div.

WA 30

CONFIDENTIAL

D.A.D.O.S.
14 DIV.

WAR DIARY.

Nov 1ˢᵗ 1917
to
Nov 30 1917.

M Henderson
D.A.D.O.S
14 Div

Army Form C. 2118

WAR DIARY
or
INTELLIGENCE SUMMARY
(Erase heading not required.)

Instructions regarding War Diaries and Intelligence Summaries are contained in F. S. Regs., Part II. and the Staff Manual respectively. Title Pages will be prepared in manuscript.

Place	Date	Hour	Summary of Events and Information	Remarks and references to Appendices
BENTHEM	9/4/17		Normal duties. Divisum out of line.	
"	2/"		Normal duties.	
"	3/"		Distribution of gloves to men in sections.	
"	4/"		No. 3 Bee on fatigue duties - forward area. No. 3 Bee at LA CLYTTE	
	5/"		Repairing roads & the Bee. at LA CLYTTE	
	6/"		Normal duties.	
"	7/"		Establishment of horse rugs being issued to units direct.	
"	8/"		Change of boots notified as from the 9th inst.	
"	9/"		Normal duties	

1875 Wt. W593/826 1,000,000 4/15 J.B.C. & A. A.D.S.S./Forms/C. 2118.

Army Form C. 2118

WAR DIARY
or
INTELLIGENCE SUMMARY
(Erase heading not required.)

Instructions regarding War Diaries and Intelligence Summaries are contained in F.S. Regs., Part II. and the Staff Manual respectively. Title Pages will be prepared in manuscript.

Place	Date	Hour	Summary of Events and Information	Remarks and references to Appendices
BERTHEN	10/11		Provision made of safety post for use of men in trenches to prevent sorts slipping to gun-butts. Arranged to hold a reserve of these posts for the purpose	
	11/11		Visits WIZERNES and arranges office and dumps	
WIZERNES	12/11		Move from BERTHEN to WIZERNES.	
	13/11		Visited new areas	
	14/11		Visited 6 R.W.S. 9	
	15/11		Nearest I.O.M. at STRAZEELE Arranged to send relocate by lorry	
	16/11		Normal duties	

1875 Wt. W593/826 1,000,000 4/15 J.B.C. & A. A.D.S.S./Forms/C. 2118.

WAR DIARY
or
INTELLIGENCE SUMMARY

(Erase heading not required.)

Army Form C. 2118

Place	Date	Hour	Summary of Events and Information	Remarks and references to Appendices
WIZERNES	17/11		Stamped raid discs with special markings and numbers. 2000 prepared in duplicate.	
	18/11		Visited 14 R.A.	
	19/11		Establishment of brigades for French & Belgian Interpreters cut down. T. Journal moved. Instructions for return of surplus cars.	
	20/11		Leave came on establishment of 7 Bn School harness 1. T. Corps School.	
	21/11		Transfer of 7 m Bn. Re-appointment cert' to O.O. Army Corps Troops. In administration.	
	22/11		Visited 8 R.B.	

WAR DIARY
or
INTELLIGENCE SUMMARY

(Erase heading not required.)

Army Form C. 2118

Place	Date	Hour	Summary of Events and Information	Remarks and references to Appendices
VIZERNES	23/11		Prepared special cover for Lewis Guns to prevent mud from entering the bearings when using gun in forward area.	
"	24/11		Normal duties.	
"	25/11		Visited Advance Depot at Bour[...]	
"	26/11		Visited 142 field Ambulance	
"	27/11		Normal duties	
"	28/11		Normal duties	
"	29/11		Units normal, for forward area	
"	30/11		Normal duties	h. Hewletson D.A.D.O.S. 4th Div.

WO 31

Confidential

WAR DIARY.

D.A.D.O.S.

14 DIV.

M. Henley
DADOS
14th Div

WAR DIARY or INTELLIGENCE SUMMARY

Army Form C. 2118

(Erase heading not required.)

Place	Date	Hour	Summary of Events and Information	Remarks and references to Appendices
WIZERNES	1/12/17		Visited new area preparatory to taking over.	
	2/12/17		Preparing to move	
	3/12/17		Took over dumps from Ord. 8" Div at VLAMERTINGHE	
VLAMERTINGHE	4/12/17		Visited 8" Div. R.A	
	5/12/17		Took over administration of 8" R.A. 8" R.E.	
	6/12/17		Commenced visiting units on inspection of watch carrying apparatus on vehicles.	
	7/12/17		Visited forward stns on Ypres Canal Bank in Bushes & area about.	

Army Form C. 2118

WAR DIARY
or
INTELLIGENCE SUMMARY
(Erase heading not required.)

Instructions regarding War Diaries and Intelligence Summaries are contained in F.S. Regs., Part II. and the Staff Manual respectively. Title Pages will be prepared in manuscript.

Place	Date	Hour	Summary of Events and Information	Remarks and references to Appendices
V.A.M.	8/12/17		Visits 43 F Ambul. see usage of cmdes allowed for Bunick. Arranges that each ambulance shoes have supply to Bunick Office as required and endent to replace. At present his Ambulance are holding their establishment of 100 gds each own. b. acting as Post Station.	
	9/12/17		Various visits	
	10/12/17		Visits A.D.M.S. VIII Corps	
	11/12/17		Visits new D.O.M.	
	12/12/17		Reviews all entries for weight & canvas shoes dial sights and RA. Cancells several items not required due to units taking over the pieces as they fitting.	

1875 Wt. W593/826 1,000,000 4/15 J.B.C. & A. A.D.S.S./Forms/C. 2118.

WAR DIARY or INTELLIGENCE SUMMARY

Army Form C. 2118

Place	Date	Hour	Summary of Events and Information	Remarks and references to Appendices
VLAMERTINGHE	13/2/17		G.O.C. visited B.A.D.S. with view to making up a fresh Gun Cover.	
	14/2/17		Visited Divisional Depot Batt'n. Inspected men coming up as reinforcements & noted underclothing & equipment.	
	15/2/17		Visited A.O.D. with view to drawing spare area stores.	
	16/2/17		Drew few item spare area stores from Base.	
	17/2/17		Noted that leather jerkins were carried for R.A. & R.E. personnel from Base whereas pack consignment of jerkins & balance of fur coats were received from Base for Infantry. It would appear that Infantry should have jerkins rather than the R.A. & R.E. Arrange to change with the Division.	

1875 Wt. W593/826 1,000,000 4/15 J.B.C. & A. A.D.S.S./Forms/C. 2118.

WAR DIARY
or
INTELLIGENCE SUMMARY
(Erase heading not required.)

Army Form C. 2118

Place	Date	Hour	Summary of Events and Information	Remarks and references to Appendices
	18/12/17		Normal duties	
	19/12/17		"	
	20/12/17		"	
	21/12/17		Visit D.A.D.O.S. 6" Bn ce move of dumps in N clay	
	22/12/17		Normal duties	
	23/12		Returns position of first cargo for horse shoes & Glycerine for Veterinary Pues and B. Respirators. Renewals and to Base & provide for this week.	
	24/12/17		Normal duties	
	25/12/17		Normal duties	

WAR DIARY
or
INTELLIGENCE SUMMARY

(Erase heading not required.)

Army Form C. 2118

Instructions regarding War Diaries and Intelligence Summaries are contained in F. S. Regs., Part II. and the Staff Manual respectively. Title Pages will be prepared in manuscript.

Place	Date	Hour	Summary of Events and Information	Remarks and references to Appendices
2	26/12/17		transportation left	
	27/12/17		Moved back to MIZERNE. DADST proceeded to No 14 Am. Depot for course	
MIZERNE	28/12		Standing out & over stores. Men arr.	
"	29/12		Men & inspection more to north camp.	
	30/12		Prepared & transport for move to his outfit. I cargo issued.	
	30/12		Normal duties	
	31/12		do	

M. Hepple/er
D.A.D.T.
1st Div

Jan 1918

Army Form C. 2118.

WAR DIARY
or
INTELLIGENCE SUMMARY.
(Erase heading not required.)

B.A.D.C.L. 14 Div — VA 32

Instructions regarding War Diaries and Intelligence Summaries are contained in F. S. Regs., Part II. and the Staff Manual respectively. Title pages will be prepared in manuscript.

Place	Date	Hour	Summary of Events and Information	Remarks and references to Appendices
1/1/18 WIZERNES	3/1/18		Units being re-equipped. Transferred from VIII to XVIII Corps	
MERICOURT	4/1/18		Division moved to MERICOURT area	
	5/1		Transferred to VII Corps	
	6/1		169 A.D.A. Bde transferred from OO Parks to no. 14 Bn. Found the unit in a very neglected condition due to many moves.	
	7/1		14 Div Arty transferred from DADOS 6" Bn to 14 Bn. Took over guns in rear area. Short of all sights and fittings.	
	8/1		Visited B.G., R.A. reference though overhauling of Art. and equipment. S.I.G.M. inspected the guns and forwarded report on same.	
	12/1		Visited Hqrs 169 A.D.A. Bde. Found units not in possession of horse rugs.	
	14/1		Transferred to III Corps	

Army Form C. 2118.

WAR DIARY
or
INTELLIGENCE SUMMARY.
(Erase heading not required.)

Instructions regarding War Diaries and Intelligence Summaries are contained in F. S. Regs., Part II. and the Staff Manual respectively. Title pages will be prepared in manuscript.

Place	Date	Hour	Summary of Events and Information	Remarks and references to Appendices
MERICOURT	14/1		Bracing of range in area. Had provision for Vermorel Sprayers, additional trucks & petrol trays, at request of D.A.D.V.S.	
	15/1		Have precautions in force. Ten G.S. wagons being used to draw stores from Railhead which was five miles away. Found horse transport quite inadequate for first few days, but a large consignment of wheels and other bulky items made transport very difficult.	
	16/1		Normal routine	
	18/1		Visited source drafts of reinforcements. Found that men from STAPLES were very badly clothed. The draft of 150 R.T.S. were in very bad condition. The clothing of men from HAVRE appeared to be satisfactory will regard to clothing.	

Army Form C. 2118.

WAR DIARY
or
INTELLIGENCE SUMMARY.

(Erase heading not required.)

Instructions regarding War Diaries and Intelligence Summaries are contained in F. S. Regs., Part II. and the Staff Manual respectively. Title pages will be prepared in manuscript.

Place	Date	Hour	Summary of Events and Information	Remarks and references to Appendices
PIENICOURT	19/1		Allocation of Lewis Gun butt catches commenced	
	21/1		News of pending move received. Visited R.E. Co's	
	23/1		Reviewed return of monthly issue to Units. Notice a marked increase in certain items of service dress, flannelette and horse shoes. Investigating?	
	24/1		Moved office to GUISCARD	
FLAVY			Moved Dump to FLAVY LE MARTEL	
			Hints on the move	
	27/1		Review of new area taken over from French Army	
			Provision made for Area O/O's	
	28/1		Office and dump move to JUSSY	
JUSSY	30/1		Visits ADST III Corps	
	31		Preparation of monthly return.	

h. henley
D.A.D.S.
29/1/18

Vol 33

Confidential

War Diary

of

D H D O S

February 1918

WAR DIARY
or
INTELLIGENCE SUMMARY.

Army Form C. 2118.

Place	Date	Hour	Summary of Events and Information	Remarks and references to Appendices
JUSSY	1/2/18		Normal routine	
	2/2		Rehearsals of Lewis Gun & Rifle exercises owing to the pieces not having been on line due to tactical reasons	
	3/2		Received Scheme for relieve of number of Batt[alion]s of a known calibre	
	4/2		Apparently a-[illegible] in Army, possibly of regiments against R.E. but in possession of own Battn. Water Pt. [illegible] drainage, Pumps, Alterations arrival of 4th 12 Scottish Rifles & the party from 1 Bn. Dubs 15th KRRL, 6 KSLI, and 5th KRRL[?].	
	6/2		Departure of 5th LA Y[eoman]r[y] and 2nd + 10th LL[?] and re-[illegible] to be distributed all of its sundries taken when on and [illegible] for paper and Rolls, Rifles [illegible] Bars and Boots checked	

Army Form C. 2118.

WAR DIARY
or
INTELLIGENCE SUMMARY.
(Erase heading not required.)

Instructions regarding War Diaries and Intelligence Summaries are contained in F. S. Regs., Part II. and the Staff Manual respectively. Title pages will be prepared in manuscript.

Place	Date	Hour	Summary of Events and Information	Remarks and references to Appendices
MISY	7/2/17		Review of Shopmeters in possession of units. Preparation of lists giving valuation and nos. of Gun Limbers	
	8/2		Normal duties	
	9/2		Visited ADOS III Corps	
	10/2		Received position as Tumber of Butter tanks with Div RE. Scrutiny of indents of attached A.S.A. Btlns. with reposculation of issues etc.	
	11/2		Packing, listing and dispatching of all surplus stores from advanced Dumps.	
	12/2		Forwarded progress report on creation of equipment of advances units to III Corps	
	13/2		Visited R.A. units	

Army Form C. 2118.

WAR DIARY
or
INTELLIGENCE SUMMARY.
(Erase heading not required.)

Instructions regarding War Diaries and Intelligence Summaries are contained in F. S. Regs., Part II. and the Staff Manual respectively. Title pages will be prepared in manuscript.

Place	Date	Hour	Summary of Events and Information	Remarks and references to Appendices
JUSSY	14/2		L.L.I. raised chocolates as to serves copies of centre arms.	
			Put this before A.O.C. Division	
	15/2		Explanation - Mailed R.S.A. units who were in a very bad condition	
			F.C. to S.C.M. No 54 + 29 workshop	
	16/2		Prepared list of suggestions with DADVS as to economy in material used in horse management.	
	17/2		Visits attended A A A Bde (169 A.F.A. Bde)	
			Visited 147 J Ambul. Inspected store of service arms	
	18/2		Tours all in order.	
	19/2		Normal routine	
			do	
	20/2		Retns Rations Auth. Gas offensive demands renewed	

Place	Date	Hour	Summary of Events and Information	Remarks and references to Appendices
MSY	21/2/18		Received position as to A.A. rifle and mountings with 6 hand of our Myn.	
	22/2		(i) Corps collects surplus tents and packsaddlery.	
	23/2		(ii) Corps O requests that hire of the four horses on our establishment be reviewed to statutory b/d. and that when necessary H.T. be used to relieve M.T. from rear.	
			Put up to G.O.C. Div. the danger of enemy M.T. from rear.	
			(iii) Q pressed us hire horses as kit s.	
	24/2		Forerunner moved to complete van with petrol behind hrs for water.	
			F Scale of 3600	
	25/2		Normal duties.	
	26		Preparation of monthly returns	
	27		Normal open routine	
	28			

W. McCalfe
D.A.D.O.S.
7th Div.

CONFIDENTIAL 1918 VR 34

WAR DIARY.

D.A.D.O.S
14 Div.

MAR 1 — 31

M. Kenton
D.A.D.O.S
14 Div

Army Form C. 2118.

WAR DIARY
or
INTELLIGENCE SUMMARY.
(Erase heading not required.)

Place	Date	Hour	Summary of Events and Information	Remarks and references to Appendices
MAR 1st -1918 JUSSY	Mar 1		Normal duty	
"	2		Normal duty	
"	3		Visit of Inspector of Armourers to 14 Div. Visited 8 K.R.R.C, 7 R.B. "SOX. & Berks I. also Divisional shops. Expressed satisfaction with condition of arms and machine guns	
"	4		Normal duty	
"	5		do	
"	6		Visited Div army of Corps Signal school at BEAUMONT EN BEINES. Arranged to make provision for equipment of school	
"	7		Visited 298 A.T.A. Bae. Surplus men sent reported to Corps	
"	8		Visited Salvage Co.	

Army Form C. 2118.

WAR DIARY
or
INTELLIGENCE SUMMARY.
(Erase heading not required.)

Instructions regarding War Diaries and Intelligence Summaries are contained in F. S. Regs., Part II. and the Staff Manual respectively. Title pages will be prepared in manuscript.

Place	Date	Hour	Summary of Events and Information	Remarks and references to Appendices
JUSSY.	9/3/18		normal duties	
"	10.		Promoes of evacuation schemes and further passwords made	
			EADOS proceeds on leave	
			Lt. LILLY M.O. O/c.	
			Evacuate his lorry loads of reserves to NOYON as not being immediately necessary. Precautionary measure.	
	11		Normal routine	
	12		do.	
	13		disturbances are Co. of 11th Kings Battl. Ohio handed it to M.O.D in front other	
	14		Evacuation reserves of Proven Battl. inspected by Corpn. Amn. Officer and returned to Base	
	15		Further stores evacuated to NOYON	

Army Form C. 2118.

WAR DIARY
or
INTELLIGENCE SUMMARY

(Erase heading not required.)

Instructions regarding War Diaries and Intelligence Summaries are contained in F.S. Regs., Part II. and the Staff Manual respectively. Title pages will be prepared in manuscript.

Place	Date	Hour	Summary of Events and Information	Remarks and references to Appendices
JUSSY	14		Visited 42" D.A inspecting equipment.	
"	17		Normal routine	
"	18		do	
"	19		do	
"	20		Visits 298 A.F.A Bde.	
"	21		Report forward s on charge of Lewis Gun butts.	
"	21		Commencement of German offensive. Shire heavily shelled. Only one lorry available with which to evacuate stores. Other this attempt made by III Corps. Planes to ADOS III Corps from XVIII Div ord. for return of this lorries. No action was taken that day. Evacuated stores to BEAUMONT by lorry loads with no lorry making several journeys. Sent to GUN PARK Jat 30 Vickers Guns. Position reported to ADOS III Corps. None available. Evacuated further on 15 Guns + Forwarn 9, 11 D.A	
"	22		Evacuated 34 - 18 PR and 12 - 4.5 howts. 4 - 4.5" How's were released by OMG 15 te aam from GUN PARK, but no transport available.	

WAR DIARY
or
INTELLIGENCE SUMMARY

Army Form C. 2118.

Place	Date	Hour	Summary of Events and Information	Remarks and references to Appendices
BEAUMONT	22/3/18		Evacuated BEAUMONT for GUISCARD. Demanded 48 Vickers Guns - None available at GUN PARK. Three lorries arrived for duty at end of day.	
GUISCARD	23/3		Evacuated GUISCARD to NOYON. Visited Bus Transport for information as to position of Lewis Guns said to be in possession.	
NOYON	24		Stragglers being re-equipped under instructions of A.P.M. III Corps. Men anxious to hold on and being handed equipment and rifles. Two lorries obtained from R.T.O. and surplus stores previously evacuated to NOYON now despatched to BAR. III Corps reported numbers of Vickers and Lewis Guns required. Estimated by even in reply 120 Lewis Guns. No further action that day. 14 D.H. demanded enough running out 18 PR Opscope & kept 20 guns in action. Obtained these from one of the 2nd Mobile Workshops.	

Army Form C. 2118.

WAR DIARY
or
INTELLIGENCE SUMMARY.
(Erase heading not required.)

Instructions regarding War Diaries and Intelligence Summaries are contained in F. S. Regs., Part II. and the Staff Manual respectively. Title pages will be prepared in manuscript.

Place	Date	Hour	Summary of Events and Information	Remarks and references to Appendices
NOYON	24/3		Evacuated NOYON 10.30 PM and proceeded to LASSIGNY. Dumped stores and retired for remainder. S/Lt Shettle in charge of last load was ordered on to NOYON before completing load. Only small detail of men personal kit attendance).	
LASSIGNY	25/3		Evacuated LASSIGNY at 5.0 am for ROSIERS-SUR-METZ. Stores again transported and lorries now attached to 14 MT unit convoy.	
ESTREES ST. DENNIS	26/3		Evacuated ROSIERES-SUR-METZ for ESTREES. ST. DENNIS. This was position of railhead, but in Shed are in position there between two outs factors. Issue of Socks, clothing made to units. Issued 20 VICKERS guns to 1st M.G. Battn from Corps reserve. 14 DIV. demanded spares and oil. Issue made from 24 lorries of belong made by Ord. to gunners in 5th DIV.	

Army Form C. 2118.

WAR DIARY
or
INTELLIGENCE SUMMARY.
(Erase heading not required.)

Instructions regarding War Diaries and Intelligence Summaries are contained in F. S. Regs., Part II. and the Staff Manual respectively. Title pages will be prepared in manuscript.

Place	Date	Hour	Summary of Events and Information	Remarks and references to Appendices
ESTREES S. DENNIS	27.		Issue to units proceeding. Each Bn. now has 20 Lewis Guns. 60 in all.	
	28.		Railhead moved to COMPIEGNE. Truck arrived but not consigned to S. ROCHE AMIENS.	
			DABDS rejoins Divisional transport at COMPIEGNE.	
	29.		Moves to PONT ST MAXENCE.	
	30.		Moves to HIBERCOURT.	
	31.		Transport on move. Re-equipment being undertaken. During the period of retirement from 21st – 28th the arrangements for supply of ordnance stores were entirely in hands of Bn. LEWY N.O.C. owing to breakdown of leave being cattle traffic was given to the Divl. Staff and at personal risk guns and vital stores were obtained and issued as required and available.	

CONFIDENTIAL. 9

1918 GR 35

WAR DIARY

DADOS
14 Div

April 1 - 30. 1918

WAR DIARY or INTELLIGENCE SUMMARY

Army Form C. 2118.

(Erase heading not required.)

Place	Date	Hour	Summary of Events and Information	Remarks and references to Appendices
HIBERCOURT	1/4/18		R.A. in action under Army control. Situation appears to [be] breaking	
	2/4		Quiet morning	
	3		Moved to SALEUX. Hqrs Divison at BOVES.	
	4		14 D.A. units re-equipped will hold return on Army.	
			20 Lewis Guns sent to reserve Amn/n 41° Bde.	
	5		16 (How) 39 B.A. moved to 2 A.D.B.D. 1st Aw.	
	6		Receipt of underclothing for bathing of all available personnel.	
	7		Reflex units on the move	
SALEUX	8		Hqrs moves to MOLINY. Transferred 16 & 39 B.A. to 5 Cav. Bde.	
	9		Re-equipping of units in progress	
	10		Hqrs moved to HOCQUELIERS	
	11		Transferred 1st B.A. to 5 Cav. Division.	

WAR DIARY
or
INTELLIGENCE SUMMARY.

(Erase heading not required.)

Army Form C. 2118.

Place	Date	Hour	Summary of Events and Information	Remarks and references to Appendices
HUCQUELIERS	12/4		Recd'd Bn. Hqrs and Batt. Hqrs for information as to where we joined "9" Scottish Rifles transferred to "9" Bn. Will be composed of Lewis Guns made up before departure. Unit is present goes on Composite Battle. may (one) of all available personnel from all the Batts. of 14 Div. It was decided to re-equip this to strength of four complete Batts. and so far as possible use natural available unit on the Battle. Position now eg:—	
			A. { 9" KRRC 5. Ox + Bucks 7 RB 11 Hus	Bn. Lg Batt to Sheiroll Hants & Dorsett complete transport
			B. { E.R.B. 9.R.B. 7 KRRC 8 KRRC Som 9 L	A. Skelton Batth Shot personnel become 1 train to A. 1. complete before and not reequipped not Stores
	14/4		Preparing for move.	

WAR DIARY
INTELLIGENCE SUMMARY
(Erase heading not required.)

Army Form C. 2118.

Place	Date	Hour	Summary of Events and Information	Remarks and references to Appendices
ECCOUIDECOUES	15/4/18		Moved to ECCOUIDECOUES. Four battr. Postigues by attached.	
	17/4		Officer opened in ECCOUIDECOUES	
	18/4		harrows duties	
	19/4		Heavy of Salvage in near villages	
	19/4		Indent EADOS Portuguese for ammunition not sufficient newary for attended work	
	20/4		Preparation for move	
	21/4		Office & new HunF opened at COYECOUES. 1st & 14 R.A. ammunition were transferred this day from Ord. S. Aml. by General dump maintained at ECCOUIDECOUES. 1st Bn about 18 9- 18RR. 7- 4.5" Hours.	
COYECOUES	22/4		Complete equipment organized by 27/28 inst.	

Army Form C. 2118.

WAR DIARY
or
INTELLIGENCE SUMMARY.
(Erase heading not required.)

Instructions regarding War Diaries and Intelligence Summaries are contained in F. S. Regs., Part II. and the Staff Manual respectively. Title pages will be prepared in manuscript.

Place	Date	Hour	Summary of Events and Information	Remarks and references to Appendices
COYECOVES	23/4		R.A recruits gunnery to all classes. Guns in use R.A.	
	24/4		Issue of Bread by mule.	
	25/4		Lorries sent twice to CALAIS for stores for R.A.	
	26/4		Normal routine. Lorries sent to GUNPARK for gun stores.	
	27/4		Lorries again sent to CALAIS for detail gun stores for R.A.	
	28/4		Section of Bty of 14 DA proceeded to line.	
			Inspected Transport of 41 + 42 Res unit 0.6 Tan 9.0 M.	
	29/4		Remainder of 14 DA proceeded to line.	
			Opened new dump for 41, 42 Bdes at WAMBER COURT.	
	29/4		Transport R.A. 15 Grand dump at ECAUDECOUES	
TORCY	30/4		Main dump moved to TORCY. 14 DA transport to O.P. 3.30.	

Siciliis

May 1918

Army Form C. 2118.

WAR DIARY
or
INTELLIGENCE SUMMARY.
(Erase heading not required.)

Instructions regarding War Diaries and Intelligence Summaries are contained in F.S. Regs., Part II. and the Staff Manual respectively. Title pages will be prepared in manuscript.

ODMS 14 5th Vol 36

Place	Date	Hour	Summary of Events and Information	Remarks and references to Appendices
TORCY.	1/5/18		Been moving to area N. of HESDIN. 36" San. Sectn. Letter transfers 1: 16 Bn.	
	2/5/18		WAMBERCOURT dump closed; COTEEQUE dump closed.	
	3/5/18		Encountered difficulty in upkeep of repairs with skeleton staff, due to lack of personnel. Arranges to report for their units to Bn. Shops.	
	4/5/18		Visits HESDIN Railhead.	
	5/5/18		Visits Inward dump at ECOIVRECOURT. Visits 41, 142 Bns. Prepares report as to losses of stores by units during with'al of armies.	
	6/5/18		Normal routine.	

Army Form C. 2118.

WAR DIARY
or
INTELLIGENCE SUMMARY.
(Erase heading not required.)

Instructions regarding War Diaries and Intelligence Summaries are contained in F. S. Regs., Part II. and the Staff Manual respectively. Title pages will be prepared in manuscript.

Place	Date	Hour	Summary of Events and Information	Remarks and references to Appendices
TORCY	6/5/18		Normal routine	
	7/5/18		S.S. Inis 60 hampers from 19 Corps to see how heads C.R.E. as to details of condition of general equipment.	
	8/5/18		Lieut. Myers & O.R. Other moved to S. QUENTIN Vt. of AIRE.	
	9/5/18		Transported to Corps reported to A.D.V.S.	
S. QUENTIN	10/5		Visited various mms hampers to BLARINGHEM	
	11/5		Trucks very slow on rail	
	12/5		Normal routine	
	12/5		do.	
	12/5		do.	

Army Form C. 2118.

WAR DIARY
or
INTELLIGENCE SUMMARY.
(Erase heading not required.)

Instructions regarding War Diaries and Intelligence Summaries are contained in F. S. Regs., Part II. and the Staff Manual respectively. Title pages will be prepared in manuscript.

Place	Date	Hour	Summary of Events and Information	Remarks and references to Appendices
S. QUENTIN	14/5		Visited Bns. and checked over important notice board.	
	15/5		Preparation of report of recent hostile breakout & outbreak of transport strike.	
	16/5		Group established at S. HENDRI FARM. W. AIRE.	
	17/5		Visits. S.A.O.T.S. Duplex Transport CUCO. reference trains & transport of advanced belt.	
	18/5		Took over administration of chstrt of 1st Belgian Div. Acts 15/6, 15/7. 60th R.G. from 16 Bn.	
	19/5		Normal routine	
	20/5		Normal routine	

Army Form C. 2118.

WAR DIARY
or
INTELLIGENCE SUMMARY.
(Erase heading not required.)

Instructions regarding War Diaries and Intelligence Summaries are contained in F. S. Regs., Part II. and the Staff Manual respectively. Title pages will be prepared in manuscript.

Place	Date	Hour	Summary of Events and Information	Remarks and references to Appendices
S. OUENTIN	21/5		Visited British mission to Portuguese. Went into details of outstanding stores with Portuguese units. Visited ADMS (withdrawn Lt. ROBERTS MOD). Visited Pantheon.	
	22/5		Normal routine	

Army Form C. 2118.

WAR DIARY
or
INTELLIGENCE/SUMMARY.
(Erase heading not required.)

Instructions regarding War Diaries and Intelligence Summaries are contained in F. S. Regs. Part II. and the Staff Manual respectively. Title pages will be prepared in manuscript.

Place	Date	Hour	Summary of Events and Information	Remarks and references to Appendices
S QUENTIN	23/5		Took over duty from Capt M.R. Neale M.C. ADD who proceeded to ENGLAND prior to going to India.	
	24/5		Visited 42nd & 43rd Brigades for Conference rushed Units of the 43rd Bdge. TRMShore	
	25/5		Inspecting Water Carts, visited Dump at Royon. Visited Rolhead at Blairgham Farm tray late arriving 3.30 pm wils	
	26/5		10 Tons of stores. General Routine	
	27/5		Attended Conference of the ADOS rediscussed the Question of economy	
	28/5		Issuing of Ordnance stores. Normal Routine Office General Routine Work visited Salvage Dump	
	29/5		Visited 42nd Brigade Headquarters, 7th KRR & 4th R.B. inspected CMShores. examined outstanding Indents	
	30/5		Cor not available, unable to visit Royon. Normal Routine	
	31/5		Normal Routine.	

H Leonard Roberts Lieut
DADOS 14th Division

29
Confidential
June 1/16. 1918

War Diary

No 37

Lt Leonard Roberts
hus
DADOS
14" Division

Army Form C. 2118.

WAR DIARY
or
INTELLIGENCE SUMMARY.
(Erase heading not required.)

Instructions regarding War Diaries and Intelligence Summaries are contained in F. S. Regs., Part II. and the Staff Manual respectively. Title pages will be prepared in manuscript.

Place	Date	Hour	Summary of Events and Information	Remarks and references to Appendices
St Rubentin	1/6/18		Visited Royers Dump, 142nd 143rd Brigade. Inspected QM Stores of all the Batts.	
	2/6/18		Visited O.C. Corps Troops. Railhead Enquedecourt. Salvage Dump also No 57 C.C.S. for books etc.	
	3/6/18		Visited 5th Royal Irish Fusiliers on their arrival from overseas to enquire as to their immediate requirements of stores etc	
	4/6/18		HDQS I Corps came spent 2 hours inspected the Dump. No cars available having been posted.	
	5/6/18		Visited Dump at Royers. General Routine. General Routine Orders 1200 Box Respirators 12600 Containers from Ranelucourt, as I was informed the 5 Battalions joining the Division from overseas had the old type Gas Appliances. General Routine.	
	6/6/18		Checked G. Field Coy. R.M. Stores. 6th Royal Inniskilling Fusiliers & 5a Royal Irish Fusiliers on their arrival.	
	7/6/18			

Army Form C. 2118.

WAR DIARY
or
INTELLIGENCE SUMMARY.
(Erase heading not required.)

Instructions regarding War Diaries and Intelligence Summaries are contained in F. S. Regs., Part II. and the Staff Manual respectively. Title pages will be prepared in manuscript.

Place	Date	Hour	Summary of Events and Information	Remarks and references to Appendices
St Quentin	8/6/18		Visited Colonels the Regt & 2/4 Connaught Rangers Depots on their arrival regarding Ordnance Stores.	
	9/6/18		Visited 6th Royal Inniskilling Fusiliers & 5th Connaught Rangers.	
	10/6/18		General Routine. No car available	
	11/6/18		General Routine. No car available	
	12/6/18		General Routine. No car available	
	13/6/18		Arranged for the transfer of Portuguese units being administered by 14th Division to be taken over by the 1st Portuguese Division at Theronanne.	
	14/6/18		Codr Bourgell 9th Regt together with all Portuguese stores outstanding debts sent by lorry to Theronanne. Received orders to prepare to move to England.	
	15/6/18		Preparing to move.	
	16/6/18		Cleared up all stores. Left for England via Boulogne.	

16/6/18

Theonard R Buchanan
D.A.D.O.S. 14th Divn

24

War Diary 6/17778
14th Division

4th/22nd July 1918

WAR DIARY or INTELLIGENCE SUMMARY

Army Form C. 2118.

Place	Date	Hour	Summary of Events and Information	Remarks and references to Appendices
Wimereux	4/7/18		Left Folkestone arrived at Boulogne thence to Wimereux Offerney arriving about 5 p.m. Rang up the ADOS 7th Corps arranged to go see him the following afternoon	
"	5/7/18		Arranged Officers notified on arrival demanded the necessary stores from Calais. Visited ADOS 7th Corps in the afternoon regarding what returns were to be rendered & for any instructions he might have	
"	6/7/18		Went to the Stationery Office at Boulogne for necessary paper etc as the Office books had not arrived. These arrived about 5.30pm. Work progressing favorably	
"	7/7/18		Visited 16th Manchester Regt "RM Stores", 43rd & 44th Field Ambulances with regard to stores & supplies of books required. General Richie	
"	8/7/18		General Richie visited Calais Depot about supplies. 3 Lorries reported for duty	
"	9/7/18		Visited Railhead regarding receipt of stores. Meeting HR 41st Infy Bdept. 33rd London Regt. 18th York Lancs Regt, Durham L.I., No 2 Coy Irrean SAH Occ 46 GHC regarding urgent requirements. General Richie	

Place	Date	Hour	Summary of Events and Information	Remarks and references to Appendices
Wimereux Etaples	10/7/18		General Routine. No Car available	
"	11/7/18		Looking for suitable Dump. After I. Walker and the GOC wished me to go there. No suitable place available, decided to go to Etaples via Boulogne. R Branch, R detail, the 3 Ordnance lorries to Camp Comdt Office at Wimereux Etaples for me. I spent 1½ whilst moving. I strongly protested and placed under "Arrest", ordered to see the GOC 9am next morning	
	12/7/18		Was interviewed by GOC 9am when he told me he was sorry for me to be removed but I was to continue to carry on until my relief arrived. In the afternoon moved half a dozen new Officer's requirement (civilians) to Etaples on one 3 cwt lorry. The 3 hire lorries being used by R Branch. The remainder will move tomorrow visited MTVS explained the situation, asked his advice thanked him my report on the subject	
Etaples	13/7/18		Visited Railhead at Walker to see if any stores had arrived. Was a store. Got some CSRs from D Corps Troops under authority of MTVS. All 3 Ordnance lorries returned Very busy making preparations to receive large quantities of stores and await movement order.	

Army Form C. 2118.

WAR DIARY
or
INTELLIGENCE SUMMARY.
(Erase heading not required.)

Instructions regarding War Diaries and Intelligence Summaries are contained in F. S. Regs., Part II. and the Staff Manual respectively. Title pages will be prepared in manuscript.

Place	Date	Hour	Summary of Events and Information	Remarks and references to Appendices
Eperlecques	14/7/18		General Routine. Four Trucks of Stores at Railhead.	
"	15/7/18		General Routine. Four Trucks of Stores at Railhead no car available	
"	16/7/18		DDOS AMOUS visited Dump regarding trouble with car Tonics. Visited 42nd Bdye HQ. 10th Highland L.I. 75th Royal North Lancs regarding clothing stores	
"	17/7/18		Visited O.C. 29th Durham L.I. & 20th Middlesex Regt regarding Paint, Boot Repairs	
"	18/7/18		Numerous General Routine	
"	19/7/18		General Routine	
"	20/7/18		General Routine	
"	21/7/18		10 Tons of Stores at Railhead General Routine. General Routine.	
"	22/7/18		Left 14th Division to proceed No 19 Ordnance Depot for ammunition course. Instructions Second Army.	

22nd July 1918

Leonard R Beck
Major
DADOS 14 Division

Army Form C. 2118.

DADOS 14
August 1918
JSL 39

WAR DIARY
or
INTELLIGENCE SUMMARY.
(Erase heading not required.)

Place	Date	Hour	Summary of Events and Information	Remarks and references to Appendices
In the Field	24th		Flue trucks cleared at Railhead — General Routine —	
"	25th		Left 30th Div and joined 14th Div vice Major L Rhodes MD to 30 Div — Inspected Dumps, salvage & Pur Ammunr's Stop.	
"	26th		Toured office from Proven to 14 Div Hqrs — Dumps still at Proven	
"	27th		Visited Dumps — Remanded Lewis Guns for S.a.a Sec for A.A. purposes — arranged to take over Dumps from DaDOS 34 Div.	
"	28th		Toured office to Poundre Camp — General Routine.	
"	29th		Toured Dumps — to the Trombecque — Boeninghe road — cleared trucks at Railhead — Received Lewis Guns for S.a.a Sec — Drew four German Machine Guns from CMR Corps troops for instructional purposes.	
"	30th		General Routine — Visited Dumps & inspected salvage.	
"	31st		Cleared trucks at Railhead — Demanded 355 sets Pack saddlery 426H pro sachs carrying, MG for Hqrs Pur Animal Pack Trans. Drew two German MG Guns from Corps Troops.	

Aremann Major
DaDOS 14 Div

Army Form C. 2118.

WAR DIARY
or
INTELLIGENCE SUMMARY.
(Erase heading not required.)

Instructions regarding War Diaries and Intelligence Summaries are contained in F. S. Regs., Part II. and the Staff Manual respectively. Title pages will be prepared in manuscript.

Place	Date	Hour	Summary of Events and Information	Remarks and references to Appendices
Farmes	26/7/18	18/1/18	At Ammunition Course Barnes	
Epelecque	7/8/18		Left ammunition Course Barnes returned to 14th Division	
"	8/8/18	11/8/18	General Routine	
"	12/8/18		7 Tons of stores General Routine	
"	13/8/18	19/8/18	General Routine	
Proven	20/8/18		Moved from Epelecque to Proven	
"	21/8/18		Completed move of shops & Mess to Proven	
"	22/8/18		General Routine	
"	23/8/18		Transferred from 14th Division to 30th Division	

23rd August 1918.

H Leonard Roberts
Major
RAVC
14th Division

DADTS/14 Army Form C. 2118.
September 1918.
Vol 40

WAR DIARY
or
INTELLIGENCE SUMMARY.
(Erase heading not required.)

Place	Date	Hour	Summary of Events and Information	Remarks and references to Appendices
In the Field	1st		General Routine: - visited #1, #2 & #3 Bde Hdqrs also Dumps. Cleared truck at Railhead	
"	2nd		DADOS in Div proceeded on leave. General Routine.	
"	3rd		General Routine - 200 sets of Packsaddlery & 160 pr Packsaddlery Packsaddlery water tins drawn from OO II Army Troops. Limbers for Dvl Pack Train	
"	4th		Cleared truck at Railhead - Issued 1444 sets Packsaddlery & 130 pr Packs carrying water tins to Infantry Bdes.	
"	5th		General Routine:- Demanded six Lewis Guns - 3 prs to APs to replace lost in action & 3 for R.E. boys as a first supply for A.A. defence. 500 Pickets tins drawn from S.M.T.O II Corps.	
"	6th		Cleared truck at Railhead. Rumours started making in doses of men in front line. 4500 required.	
"	7th		General Routine. - Received six Lewis Guns from Gun Park 3 issued to 13th APS & one to acct Fd Coy R.E. - Salvage returned to Railhead.	
"	8th		Cleared truck at Railhead. - Orders received to move Dump. New place selected.	

Army Form C. 2118.

WAR DIARY
or
INTELLIGENCE SUMMARY.

(Erase heading not required.)

September 1918

Place	Date	Hour	Summary of Events and Information	Remarks and references to Appendices
In the Field	9th		General Routine. Cleared truck at Railhead. Collected Biscuit tins from Lefèbres Pants for making tins discs	
"	10th		Drew 40 Boxes Belt for German M.G. Guns from OO II Corps Troops. General Routine.	
"	11th		Cleared truck at Railhead. Collected biscuit tins from A.S.C. Coys. – Divisional Armourers Shoemakers & Tailors Shops inspected. General Routine.	
"	12th		Drew 300 suits of Service Dress from Corps Troops to provide men with a dry change when coming out of the line in a wet condition. – General Routine.	
"	13th		Cleared truck at Railhead. Stored Dumps to Aerodrome on the Couture - Vijezenzele Road. General Routine.	
"	14th		General Routine. Arrahands made in Labour Shops for E.O.S.3. Chaffcutter demanded through Corps for issue to the 42 Inf Bde.	

Army Form C. 2118.

WAR DIARY
or
INTELLIGENCE SUMMARY.
(Erase heading not required.)

September 1918

Place	Date	Hour	Summary of Events and Information	Remarks and references to Appendices
In the Field	15th		Cleared truck at Railhead. - Sent stores to Refilling Point - for 42 Bde at Runzeele - General Routine.	
"	16th		Armourers shop completed 1000 bin discs. - Drew 265 B.Rs fitted with American Cloth from Corps Troops. - General Routine	
"	17th		Cleared truck at Railhead - General Routine.	
"	18th		General Routine - This sent to Refilling Point for 42 Bde. Demanded one complete Vickers Gun for 14th N.F. Battn.	
"	19th		Cleared truck at Railhead. - Drew 50 sets pack saddlery & 100 Dato Carriers from OO 2nd Army Troops No 3. LUMBRES & 290 Ammn. Carriers 18 pdr & 120 Carriers 4.5 how from No 2 Army Gun Park at WATTEN. - Four Stores foyer & 21 Inks Dashers drawn from Corps Troops for Foot treatment.	
"	20th		Stores Office & Dump Sheet 27 L 23 a 7.7 nr Bavinghe - Closed truck at Railhead. - Demanged two 18 pdr for S/h/T. 14th Park Artillery, moved from Depot 19, Div fis 14th Div - W.O. a/c 14th D.A. arrived.	

WAR DIARY or INTELLIGENCE SUMMARY

Army Form C. 2118.

September 1918

Place	Date	Hour	Summary of Events and Information	Remarks and references to Appendices
In the Field	21st		2000 petrol tins drawn from R.S.O. Dickebusch. also 200 Carriers Amm. Emergency path 18 pdrs from O.O. 2nd Army Gun Park. WATTEN. General Routine.	
"	22nd		300 bekot tins, 100 Carriers Emergency bath 18 pdrs & 400 Carriers 18pdr 4.5 Hows issued to 14 Divl Artillery. Three Carriages 18pdr returned by I.O.M. & demanded for S/47.Bde. — Two 18pdrs issued to S/47.	
"	23rd		Three extra Tailors arrived from 41 Bde. to help make 235 Maps fitted with white American Cloth for S.B.R's. Tailors Shop made 150 yellow + 50 Intelligence arm bands — Armourers Shop completed 3000 tin cases — Packsaddlery & Petrol tins delivered to Bomb Store OUDERDOM. — Three Lewis Guns demanded. Three Carriages 18pdr issued to S/47.	
"	24th		100 flaps for S.B.R's complete in Tailors Shop. — Three Lewis Guns received from Gun Park. — 400 bekot tins. St sep H Packsaddlery & 50 prs Jacks carrying sandgs delivered 15 Bomb to OUDERDOM — 1856 tin cases issued to 41 Bde. S.P. Bde.	
"	25th		Closed truck at Railhead. Issued 1200 tin cases to 42 Inf Bde & 60 to 43 Bde. Demanded A.S. Hows for D/46 Bde. General Routine.	

Army Form C. 2118.

WAR DIARY
or
INTELLIGENCE SUMMARY.

(Erase heading not required.)

September 1918

Instructions regarding War Diaries and Intelligence Summaries are contained in F. S. Regs., Part II. and the Staff Manual respectively. Title pages will be prepared in manuscript.

Place	Date	Hour	Summary of Events and Information	Remarks and references to Appendices
In the field	26th		General Routine. - Vickers Gun demanded for 14 T.S. Batty. - 235 S.B.R's fitted with white American Cloth completed in favors also - 50 Electric torches purchased at St. Omer also 110 yellow armbands. for Special Operations.	
"	27th		Observed truck at Railhead. - Vickers Gun received from Gun Park. General Routine.	
"	28th		General Routine. - Demanded Wagon 8mm 18 pdr for Dept Bde	
"	29th		General Routine. Two lorry loads of Salvage returned to Railhead. - Inspected Divnson Workshops. -	
"	30th		Observed truck at Railhead. - returned Salvage to Railhead. Offr. advised to draw Wagon 8mm 18pdr from 1 to 12 Workshops. General Routine.	

30/9/18

Command Major
DADOS 14 Div

Army Form C. 2118.

WAR DIARY
or
INTELLIGENCE SUMMARY.
(Erase heading not required.)

October 1918

M.T. A.D.S.

Place	Date	Hour	Summary of Events and Information	Remarks and references to Appendices
In the Field	1st		Cleared truck at Railhead. Collected Packsaddlery & Water Carriers from Bomb store at OUDERDOM.	
"	2nd		General Routine. Delivered 118 sets Packsaddlery & 48 prs Water Carriers to H1 Bde.	
"	3rd		General Routine. Stored Dump. To Steenvoorde Eglise & Office to Waratah Camp nr. Poperinghe.	
"	4th		Cleared truck at Railhead. Visited Dump & arranged Refilling Points.	
"	5th		Cleared truck at Railhead. General Routine.	
"	6th		General Routine. Demanded 16,200 Drawers & 11,100 Vests from Base.	
"	7th		Cleared truck at Railhead. Demanded Six Lewis Guns for 6 Wks & two for 14th A.S. Sights.	
"	8th		General Routine. Received Lewis Guns for 6 Wks & 14 A.S. Sights.	
"	9th		Cleared truck at Railhead. Ltd Ammunition Carriers 18,000 + A.S. Short to Gun Park. Stored Office from Waratah Camp to CAESTRE	

Army Form C. 2118.

WAR DIARY
or
INTELLIGENCE SUMMARY.
(Erase heading not required.)

October 1918

Place	Date	Hour	Summary of Events and Information	Remarks and references to Appendices
In the Field	10th		General Routine. Demanded 1 L. Gun for 29 D.L.I. & 1 Vickers for 14 J.S. Battn.	
"	11th		Cleared truck at Railhead. Received 11,000 Drawers & 6000 Vests from Base. Visited Dumps.	
"	12th		General Routine. Demanded 1 L. Gun for 20th Middlesex Regt.	
"	13th		General Routine.	
"	14th		Cleared truck at Railhead. Visited Dumps.	
"	15th		General Routine. Demanded Wagon limb G.S. for 61st Fd Coy R.E.	
"	16th		Cleared truck at Railhead. Received 5000 Drawers & 4000 Vests from Base.	
"	17th		Moved Office from CAESTRE to 28/T.1.C.6.2 on NEUVE EGLISE	
"	18th		Cleared truck at Railhead. Received 520 pr Boots F.S. from Base.	
"	19th		General Routine.	
"			Moved Office to Kandahah Camp: demanded complete Travelling Kitchen for 6th Welch Regt.	

Army Form C. 2118.

WAR DIARY
or
INTELLIGENCE SUMMARY.
(Erase heading not required.)

October 1918

Place	Date	Hour	Summary of Events and Information	Remarks and references to Appendices
In the Field	20th		Moved Office from Kandahar Camp to Le Blanc Four - General Routine (28/T.10.F.88)	
"	21st		Cleared truck at Railhead - Sent stores to Refilling Points.	
"	22nd		Moved Office to Souveron & Dump from Neuve Eglise to Le Blanc Four - General Routine.	
"	23rd		General Routine - visited Dumps & inspected Workshops - demanded Lewis Gun for 18th York & Lancs	
"	24th		Cleared truck at Railhead - received Gun for 18th York Lancs	
"	25th		Moved Dump to Ferseux & cleared seven trucks at Railhead. General Routine	
"	26th		General Routine - Cleared trucks at Railhead. Issued Winter Clothing	
"	27th		Sent in lorry loads of Salvage to Railhead - assisted Dumps.	
"	28th		General Routine - cleared truck at Railhead - Received 300 Horse Rugs & demanded 1800 for Stab Bde R.F.A.	

Army Form C. 2118.

WAR DIARY
or
INTELLIGENCE SUMMARY.
(Erase heading not required.)

October 1918

Place	Date	Hour	Summary of Events and Information	Remarks and references to Appendices
In the field	29th		General Routine. Demanded two 18 pdr Guns for 8/146 & B/146 Bde RFA - Tested Pump.	
" "	30th		Cleared truck at Railhead - three lorry loads of Salvage returned to Railhead - 160 Tents & ~300 Shelters returned by trucks in bad condition at Dump.	
" "	31st		General Routine - Four lorry loads Salvage returned to Railhead. Issues of Winter Clothing being made to Units of Div.	

Ammunt
Major
DADOS 14 Div

D.A.D.O.S.
H.Q.
14th DIVISION
No. 3/11/10/18
Date

Army Form C. 2118.

WAR DIARY
or
INTELLIGENCE SUMMARY.
(Erase heading not required.)

DADOS 14
November 1918

Place	Date	Hour	Summary of Events and Information	Remarks and references to Appendices
In the field	1st		General Routine. - Cleared truck at Railhead.	
"	2nd		General Routine. - Returned 80 Tubs & 287 Shelters to Corps. Salvage Dump LANNOY.	
"	3rd		Cleared truck at Railhead. - Demanded Cab Buts from 29 Div & OGS 18 prs & BM for Bn 46. - Issued 4000 Nuts to Batts.	
"	4th		General Routine. - Board Office from MOUSCRON to TOURCOING. Returned 119 Tubs, 1 Traverse & 3 Tarpaulins to Corps Salvage Dump.	
"	5th		Cleared truck at Railhead. Demanded Wagon for GS complete for 61 Fld Co RE - returned Salvage to Railhead.	
"	6th		General Routine. - Visited Dumps & inspected Div Workshops.	
"	7th		Cleared truck at Railhead - collected 1850 Blankets from DADOS 29 Div. General Routine.	
"	8th		General Routine. - Demanded Vickers Gun for 1st Sea Bn Butts	
"	9th		Cleared truck at Railhead - demanded two Lewis Guns for 18th York Regt	

Army Form C. 2118.

WAR DIARY
or
INTELLIGENCE SUMMARY.
(Erase heading not required.)

November 1918

Place	Date	Hour	Summary of Events and Information	Remarks and references to Appendices
In the field	10th		General Routine - worked Dump inspected Salvage returned by Units.	
" "	11th		General Routine - Cleared truck at Railhead. Received Lewis Guns for 18th York Lancs. - Babus proceeded to Paris on duty	
" "	12th		General Routine - Cleared & Trucks at Railhead, including 10,500 Blankets. Visited Dump Workshops.	
" "	13th		General Routine - Returned two lorry loads of Salvage to Railhead	
" "	14th		Cleared truck at Railhead - visited Dump & Workshops.	
" "	15th		General Routine - Completed issues of 2nd Blanket.	
" "	16th		Cleared truck at Railhead - retd 18, 18 pdr, & 20 H.S. Short emergency Ammunition carriers to Base reported numbers to XV Corps.	
" "	17th		General Routine - retd Salvage to Railhead - received 105 sets of Packsaddlery.	

Army Form C. 2118.

WAR DIARY
or
INTELLIGENCE SUMMARY.

(Erase heading not required.)

November 1918.

Place	Date	Hour	Summary of Events and Information	Remarks and references to Appendices
In the Field	18th		General Routine - Cleared truck at Railhead - erected Dump.	
" "	19th		General Routine - 212 ok Packsaddling + 159 pro Rokes carrying water. Lieut returned to Base.	
" "	20th		General Routine - Dadus returned from Paris - Cleared truck at Railhead.	
" "	21st		General Routine - erected Dump - sold Salvage to Railhead.	
" "	22nd		General Routine - selected new Dump at TOURCOING - Cleared truck at Railhead.	
" "	23rd		General Routine - Dump moved to PLACE THIERS, TOURCOING. Cleared truck at Railhead - Demanded two guns for 646 Bde. R.F.A. (not inaccuracy)	
" "	24th		General Routine - Completing move of Dump from HERSEAUX to TOURCOING - Base Cat gazetted, advised inability to accept Stores and Salvage.	
" "	25th		General Routine - Worked Dump - Cleared truck at Railhead.	
" "	26th		General Routine - Despatched four 3 ton lorry loads of Salvage and surplus stores to Railhead Disposal Dump.	

Army Form C. 2118.

WAR DIARY
or
INTELLIGENCE SUMMARY.
(Erase heading not required.)

November 1918

Place	Date	Hour	Summary of Events and Information	Remarks and references to Appendices
In the Field	27.		General Routine - Visited Dump - Issued Two 18-pdrs to 64th A.B. Ag Bde Army R.F.A with 407, 408, 409 & 410 Btys moved to 14th Divn for Ordnance services from XV Corps Troops "B"	
— " —	28.		General Routine - Visited Dump and Workshops - Salvage returned to Railhead	
— " —	29.		General Routine - Cleared Truck at Railhead - 100 yards F.S. drawn from XV Corps Troops "A" for Kittels and Retreats	
— " —	30.		General Routine - Visited Dump and Workshops - Salvage to Railhead	

30/11/18

[signature]
Major
DADOS
14th Division

Army Form C. 2118.

WAR DIARY
or
INTELLIGENCE SUMMARY.
(Erase heading not required.)

DADS 14
December 1918
CRS 143

Place	Date	Hour	Summary of Events and Information	Remarks and references to Appendices
Sheet 19	1st		General Routine - Salvage Returned to Railhead.	
-,,-	2nd		General Routine - Cleared 12 tons General stores from Railhead - Visited Dump and Workshops.	
-,,-	3rd		General Routine - Visited Dump & Workshops - Demanded 083. 18 fur sor + cattle	
-,,-	4th		General Routine - Returned Salvage to Railhead - Cleared truck new Drainage from Railhead	
-,,-	5th		General Routine - Armourers commenced touring Battalions for the Overhaul of Lewis Guns &c.	
-,,-	6th		General Routine - Returned Salvage to Railhead - Cleared truck of new stores from Base.	
-,,-	7th		General Routine - Visited Workshops and Dump - Ordered stores from Tank No. 5. sent to Workshops ROUBAIX.	
-,,-	8th		General Routine - Returned Salvage to Railhead - cleared truck new stores from Base - Visited Dump.	
-,,-	9th		General Routine - Cleared truck of Railhead.	
-,,-	10th		General Forage - drew 1500 Rations from Corps Troops received to	

Army Form C. 2118.

WAR DIARY
or
INTELLIGENCE SUMMARY.

(Erase heading not required.)

December 1918

Instructions regarding War Diaries and Intelligence Summaries are contained in F. S. Regs., Part II. and the Staff Manual respectively. Title pages will be prepared in manuscript.

Place	Date	Hour	Summary of Events and Information	Remarks and references to Appendices
In the Field	11th		General Routine – cleared 100 knots at Railhead – retd Salvage to Base – inspected Dub. Both's L.G.S.	
"	12th		General Routine – Armourers inspected Lewis Guns of the 10th R.I.	
"	13th		General Routine – cleared truck at Railhead – retd Salvage to Base	
"	14th		General Routine – cleared truck at Railhead	
"	15th		General Routine – Salvage ret'd to Railhead – Armourers inspected Lewis Guns of the 18th York Lancs.	
"	16th		General Routine – cleared truck at Railhead	
"	17th		Collected 1000 Blankets from Courtrai for issue as 3rd Blanket per man	
"	18th		General Routine – collected 3780 Blankets from Courtrai. retd Salvage to Railhead.	

Army Form C. 2118.

WAR DIARY
or
INTELLIGENCE SUMMARY.

(Erase heading not required.)

December 1918

Place	Date	Hour	Summary of Events and Information	Remarks and references to Appendices
In the Field	19th		General Routine. - Cleared truck at Railhead. -	
" "	20th		General Routine - retd salvage to Railhead. -	
" "	21st		General Routine - Orders received to move Dumps new place selected.	
" "	22nd		General Routine - cleared 20 Stores Lorrys from Railhead.	
" "	23rd		General Routine - cleared truck at Railhead - retd salvage 15 Railhead. - Stored Dump 16 Rue Turenne. Tournering	
" "	24th		General Routine - collected 150 Lamps from Corps Troops -	
" "	25th		General Routine.	
" "	26th		General Routine. - cleared truck at Railhead. -	
" "	27th		General Routine - retd Salvage to Railhead - inspected Dul SLPs.	

Army Form C. 2118.

WAR DIARY
or
INTELLIGENCE SUMMARY.

(Erase heading not required.)

December 1918

Place	Date	Hour	Summary of Events and Information	Remarks and references to Appendices
In the Field	28th		General Routine - Cleared truck at Railhead - sent salvage to Railhead	
" "	29th		General Routine - Inspected Div Workshops - collected 2000 Paillasses from Corps Troops.	
" "	30th		General Routine - Cleared truck at Railhead.	
" "	31st		General Routine - Collected two lorry loads of stores from Corps depot. Sent for transmission to Base.	

Allenought
Major
DADOS 14th Div

D.A.D.O.S.
H.Q.
14th DIVISION
31/12/18

DADOS 14b

Army Form C. 2118.

WAR DIARY
or
INTELLIGENCE SUMMARY.
(Erase heading not required.)

January 1919.

Place	Date	Hour	Summary of Events and Information	Remarks and references to Appendices
In the Field	1st		General Routine - Cleared truck at Railhead - retd Salvage to Railhead.	
"	2nd		General Routine - Inspected Divl Bath Slops.	
"	3rd		General Routine - Cleared truck at Railhead - retd Salvage to Railhead	
"	4th		General Routine - Received 5100 socks from Base for the Divl Baths	
"	5th		General Routine - cleared truck at Railhead - inspected Divl Slops	
"	6th		General Routine - retd Salvage to Railhead.	
"	7th		General Routine - Demanded 5000 sets of underclothing from Base as Divl turnover at Baths.	
"	8th		General Routine - Received balance of 3rd Blanket from Base to complete Divn to full establishment.	
"	9th		General Routine - cleared truck at Railhead - Drew 200 Braziers from Corps Troops & 40 Bicycles received from Canteens.	

Army Form C. 2118.

WAR DIARY
or
INTELLIGENCE SUMMARY.
(Erase heading not required.)

January 1919

Instructions regarding War Diaries and Intelligence Summaries are contained in F. S. Regs., Part II. and the Staff Manual respectively. Title pages will be prepared in manuscript.

Place	Date	Hour	Summary of Events and Information	Remarks and references to Appendices
In the Field	10th		General Routine - Cleared truck at Railhead.	
"	11th		General Routine - Field Salvage to Railhead - Inspected Divil Workshops	
"	12th		General Routine - Collected stores from Senin which were left behind by 2nd Army R.A. Reinforcement Camp.	
"	13th		General Routine - Cleared truck at Railhead - Sold Salvage to Base	
"	14th		General Routine - Collected stores from Railhead for Corps Horse Shoeing Camp & delivered them to Busit Factory, Tourcoing.	
"	15th		General Routine - Cleared truck at Railhead - demanded 80 T 18 pdrs for A/146 Bde R.F.A. - condemned by I.O.M.	
"	16th		General Routine - Inspected Divisional Workshops - demanded Carriage Q.F. 15 pdrs for A/146 condemned by I.O.M.	

Army Form C. 2118.

WAR DIARY
or
INTELLIGENCE SUMMARY.
(Erase heading not required.)

January 1919

Place	Date	Hour	Summary of Events and Information	Remarks and references to Appendices
In the Field	17th		General Routine - Cleared truck at Railhead - Took over duties as A.D.O.S. - Capt Smith acting as Base S.	
"	18th		General Routine. Demanded nine Lewis Guns for F.A. Corps F.E. to complete to establishment of F.S 1098.	
"	19th		General Routine. Cleared truck at Railhead returned Salvage to Railhead.	
"	20 "		General Routine - collected stores from Railheads for Cobb's Shops, camps & returned them to Bomb Factory workshop.	
"	21st		General Routine - tested sheds of 441 Inf Bde for storing Salvage & Ration Stores.	
"	22nd		General Routine - Cleared truck at Railhead - Visited Corps Troops "B". & inspected Workshops	
"	23 "		General Routine	

WAR DIARY
or
INTELLIGENCE SUMMARY.
(Erase heading not required.)

Army Form C. 2118.

January 1919

Place	Date	Hour	Summary of Events and Information	Remarks and references to Appendices
Lille Sth	24		General Routine - Cleared truck at Railhead	
"	25		General Routine - Demanded two OQF 18 pdr for B/46, one OQF 18 pdr for C/47, one OQF 45 rounds for B/46 also one Carriage 18 pdr for C/47.	
"	26		General Routine - Cleared truck at Railhead. Demanded 45 rounds for D/47, 18 pdr, for C/46, and 18 pdr for A/47 Bde RFA	
"	27		General Routine - Demanded one 18 pdr for Hqt Bty, 96 Bde, also one Carriage OQF 18 pdr for HQ Bty 96 Bde.	
"	28		General Routine - Cleared truck at Railhead -	
"	29		General Routine - Demanded One OQF 18 pdr for 410 Bty 96 Bde RFA	
"	30		General Routine - Demanded Two OQF 18 pdr for 410 Bty 96 Bde RFA, also one Carriage 18 pdr for C/47 Bde RFA	
"	31		General Routine	

Capt
for DaDOS 14 Div

Army Form C. 2118.

WAR DIARY
or
INTELLIGENCE SUMMARY.

DADOS 14 February 1919

Place	Date	Hour	Summary of Events and Information	Remarks and references to Appendices
In the Field	1st		General Routine. Retd Salvage to Railhead. Inspected Bn Workshops	
	2nd		General Routine - Cleared trucks at Railhead - Demanded 18 pdrs for 410 Bty, Two 18 pdrs for 408 Bty, One 18 pdr, 407 & 134, Two 18 pdrs for 409 Bty	
	3rd		General Routine - Demanded One 18 pdr each for 410 & 408 Bty, 96 Bde.	
	4th		General Routine - Cleared truck at Railhead -	
	5th		General Routine - Inspected Sheds selected by Subs for Subjugation Stores.	
	6th		General Routine - Cleared truck at Railhead.	
	7th		General Routine - Inspected Divisional Workshops, Tuboro & Armourers Shops.	

WAR DIARY
or
INTELLIGENCE SUMMARY.
(Erase heading not required.)

Army Form C. 2118.

February 1919

Place	Date	Hour	Summary of Events and Information	Remarks and references to Appendices
In the Field	8th		General Routine – Cleared two trucks at Railhead –	
"	9th		General Routine. Arrangements made re Stores Stationery for Intermediate Collecting Stations when Demobilization is ordered.	
"	10th		General Routine – Closed down Dyit. Tailors Bootmakers Shops owing to all men to Shops being demobilized.	
"	11th		General Routine – Cleared two trucks at Railhead – received nine Lewis Guns for R.E. Corps	
"	12th		General Routine – Received from Base two trucks loads of Saddlery for Corps Horse Staging Camps.	
"	13th		General Routine.	
"	14th		General Routine	

Army Form C. 2118.

WAR DIARY
or
INTELLIGENCE SUMMARY.
(Erase heading not required.)

February 1919

Place	Date	Hour	Summary of Events and Information	Remarks and references to Appendices
Lake Tull	15th		General Routine. Cleared truck at Railhead. Demanded for Nose Bags Saddlery for Corps Staging Camps.	
"	16th		General Routine - Cleared truck at Railhead.	
"	17th		General Routine - New dump found for Salvage owing to congestion in Dump - Base unable to accept Salvage.	
"	18th		General Routine - Mob landing in clothing machines to provide boot at Corps Troops.	
"	19th		General Routine - Sent 20 GS Wagons to Railhead to clear three trucks. Owing to frost precautions - no lorries running.	
"	20th		General Routine - Delivered stores to Staging Corps Fair Rouselles, Contrai & Senin.	
"	21st		General Routine - Cleared truck at Railhead.	

Army Form C. 2118.

WAR DIARY
or
INTELLIGENCE SUMMARY.
(Erase heading not required.)

February 1919

Place	Date	Hour	Summary of Events and Information	Remarks and references to Appendices
In the Field	22nd		General Routine - Returned three lorry loads of Salvage to Railhead.	
"	23"		General Routine - returned three lorry loads of Salvage to Railhead -	
"	24		General Routine - Cleared two trucks at Railhead ret'd three lorry loads of Salvage to Base.	
"	25		General Routine - Cleared two trucks at Railhead, including 900 tubs Dubbing.	
"	26		General Routine - Ret'd Salvage to Railhead -	
"	27		General Routine. Ret'd Salvage to Railhead - Issued stores to Corps Signal Coys.	
"	28		General Routine - Cleared truck at Railhead ret'd Salvage to Base	Mhunt Capt for ADOS in Div

Army Form C. 2118.

WAR DIARY
or
INTELLIGENCE SUMMARY.
(Erase heading not required.)

March 1919

Place	Date	Hour	Summary of Events and Information	Remarks and references to Appendices
In the Field	1st		General Routine - Cleared truck at Railhead	
"	2nd		General Routine - Auto Incident - Bicycles allowed in O/Store Tattoo	
"	3rd		General Routine - Cleared truck at Railhead	
"	4th		General Routine - Capt A.P. Smith left 14th Div to join 11th Div as DADOS.	
"	5th		General Routine - Cleared truck at Railhead.	
"	6th		General Routine - Keith three lorry loads of Salvage to Base	
"	7th		General Routine - Cleared truck at Railhead - sent three lorry loads of Salvage to Base.	

Army Form C. 2118.

WAR DIARY
or
INTELLIGENCE SUMMARY.
(Erase heading not required.)

March 1919

Place	Date	Hour	Summary of Events and Information	Remarks and references to Appendices
In the field	8th		General Routine - Old Free lorry loads of Salvage to Railhead	
—	9th		General Routine - Cleared truck at Railhead.	
—	10th		General Routine - Lieut Simonds Asst Inspector of Arms reported to Division	
—	11th		General Routine - Cleared truck at Railhead - Rifles & Lee Guns inspected of the 18th York Lancs	
—	12th		General Routine - Rifles & Lec Guns of the 29th DLI inspected	
—	13th		General Routine - Cleared truck at Railhead - Rifles & Lec Guns of 33 London Reg inspected	
—	14th		General Routine - sent 14 lorry loads of Salvage to Base	
—	15th		General Routine - Took over duties as Inspecting Officer XV Corps, Salvage Equipment Depot entraining for embarkation to clothing units England.	

WAR DIARY
or
INTELLIGENCE SUMMARY.

Army Form C. 2118.

March 1919

Place	Date	Hour	Summary of Events and Information	Remarks and references to Appendices
In Field	16th		General Routine – Inspected Stk Equipment of 7 Siege Battery R.G.A. Cleared truck at Railhead.	
"	17th		General Routine – Checked Stk Equipment of 33 Siege Bty, 39th T.S. Bdm – 2 Bde Negro R.G.A.	
"	18th		General Routine – Cleared truck at Railhead.	
"	19th		General Routine. Rec'd 11,180 Guns from Base Stk Equipment of the 14th T.S. Bdm.	
"	20th		General Routine – Cleared truck at Railhead.	
"	21st		General Routine.	
"	23		General Routine – Cleared truck at Railhead.	
"	24		General Routine – Inspected Stk Equipment of 2nd Royal Innis Fus & 1st Royal Irish Rifles.	

WAR DIARY
or
INTELLIGENCE SUMMARY.

(Erase heading not required.)

Army Form C. 2118.

March 1919

Place	Date	Hour	Summary of Events and Information	Remarks and references to Appendices
In the Field	25		General Routine. — Rifles & Mac. Guns of 10th H.L.I. inspected	
"	26		General Routine — Rifles & Mac. Guns of 12th Suffolk Rgt inspected	
"	27		General Routine	
"	28		General Routine — Tow trailer Bicycles dispatched to Havrincourt (Hospices)	
"	29		General Routine — Stores removed to Marcoing — Rifles & Mac. Guns of D/14 Bde inspected.	
"	30		General Routine	
"	31		General Routine. — Rifles and Mac. Guns of 15th L.N. Lancs inspected	

Armament
Major
D.A.D.O.S.

D.A.D.O.S.,
H.Q.,
14th DIVISION.

Army Form C. 2118.

WAR DIARY
or
INTELLIGENCE SUMMARY.
(Erase heading not required.)

STAPS 14D April 1919 Vol 47

Place	Date	Hour	Summary of Events and Information	Remarks and references to Appendices
In the Field	1st	—	General Routine — 76 Bicycles despatched to Hoymille. Rifles and Mach. Guns of 62nd & 89th Field bgs. inspected.	
"	2nd	—	General Routine — Rifles and Mac. Guns of 11th D.A.C. inspected (all Services)	
"	3rd	—	General Routine — Rifles and Mgn Guns of 46 Bde inspected — 2000 Men Regs despatched to Paris	
"	4th	—	General Routine — Rifles and Mgc Guns of 9th Bde A.F.A. inspected.	
"	5th	—	General Routine —	
"	6th	—	General Routine —	
"	7th	—	General Routine — 90 Bicycles despatched to Hoymille	

Army Form C. 2118.

WAR DIARY
or
INTELLIGENCE SUMMARY.

(Erase heading not required.)

April 1919

Place	Date	Hour	Summary of Events and Information	Remarks and references to Appendices
Anfield	8th		General Routine.	
—	9th		General Routine.	
—	10th		General Routine — 2,650 Horse Rugs despatched to Calais	
—	11th		General Routine	
—	12th		General Routine	
—	13th		General Routine	
—	14th		General Routine	

Army Form C. 2118.

WAR DIARY
or
INTELLIGENCE SUMMARY.
(Erase heading not required.)

April 1919

Instructions regarding War Diaries and Intelligence Summaries are contained in F. S. Regs., Part II. and the Staff Manual respectively. Title pages will be prepared in manuscript.

Place	Date	Hour	Summary of Events and Information	Remarks and references to Appendices
In the Field	15th		General Routine. Lorries clearing Corps Troops I.C.S.	
	16th		General Routine. Lorries clearing Corps Troops I.C.S. Visited 38th Division	
	17th		General Routine. — do —	
	18th		General Routine. — do —	
	19th		General Routine.	
	20th		General Routine. Lorries clearing C. Troops I.C.S.	
	21st		General Routine. — do —	

Army Form C. 2118.

WAR DIARY
or
INTELLIGENCE SUMMARY.
(Erase heading not required.)

Instructions regarding War Diaries and Intelligence Summaries are contained in F. S. Regs. Part II. and the Staff Manual respectively. Title pages will be prepared in manuscript.

April 1919

Place	Date	Hour	Summary of Events and Information	Remarks and references to Appendices
In the Field	22nd		General Routine. Lorries clearing Corps Salvage Dump	
—	23rd		General Routine — do —	
—	24th		General Routine — do —	
—	25th		General Routine — do —	
—	26th		General Routine — do —	
—	27th		General Routine.	
—	28th		General Routine. Lorries clearing Corps Salvage Dump. Inspected Mob. Equipment of 2nd Cavalry Division Reserve Pk & Cavalry Corps Reserve Pk.	

Army Form C. 2118.

WAR DIARY
or
INTELLIGENCE SUMMARY.
(Erase heading not required.)

April 1919

Place	Date	Hour	Summary of Events and Information	Remarks and references to Appendices
In the Field	29th		General Routine. — Inspected Mot. Equipment of 160 Hy Bty, R.G.A.	
	30th		General Routine. — Inspected Mot. Equipment of 43 T. Dis M.C., 12th Suffolk R., 20 Middlesex Rgt., 10th Highland L.Infy.	

D.A.D.O.S.
H.Q.
14th DIVISION.
No.............
Date...........

DADOS 14D

May 1919

WAR DIARY
or
INTELLIGENCE SUMMARY
(Erase heading not required.)

Army Form C. 2118.

Place	Date	Hour	Summary of Events and Information	Remarks and references to Appendices
In the Field	1st		General Routine — Inspected M/T. Equipment of 898 Field Coy. 401 Bde H.Q. & 33rd L.T.R. Bde.	
—	2nd		General Routine — Inspected M.T. Equipment of 43rd Field Ambulance and 64 M.G.S. Regt.	
—	3rd		General Routine — Aff. Sep Div ? 18th I.Y. Corps, 62nd Field Engr. 44th Field Ambce. M/T. Equipment inspected	
—	4th		General Routine	
—	5th		General Routine — 145 A.T.S. H.Qrs and 136 Army Troops Coy R.E. M/T. Equipment inspected	
—	6th		General Routine — 29th Divn A.T. and 15 & N. Lorries M/T. Equipment inspected	
—	7th		General Routine —	

a

Army Form C. 2118.

WAR DIARY
or
INTELLIGENCE SUMMARY.
(Erase heading not required.)

May 1917

Instructions regarding War Diaries and Intelligence Summaries are contained in F. S. Regs., Part II. and the Staff Manual respectively. Title pages will be prepared in manuscript.

Place	Date	Hour	Summary of Events and Information	Remarks and references to Appendices
In the field	8th		Shot Equipment of 154th & 156th Heavy Bty R.F.A. were inspected.	
	9th		General Routine	
	10th		General Routine	
	11th		Collecting stores from Sub Area R.E. Dump & lending same to Corps M.G.S. at Muxerow	
	12th		General Routine	do
	13th		General Routine	do
	14th		General Routine	do

Army Form C. 2118.

WAR DIARY
or
INTELLIGENCE SUMMARY.
(Erase heading not required.)

May 1919

Instructions regarding War Diaries and Intelligence Summaries are contained in F. S. Regs., Part II. and the Staff Manual respectively. Title pages will be prepared in manuscript.

Place	Date	Hour	Summary of Events and Information	Remarks and references to Appendices
In the Field	15th		General Routine.	
	16th		General Routine. Mob. Equipment of 23rd Lohokari Regt. 8th Road Inst. Regt. & 219th Siege Bty. were inspected.	
	17th		General Routine. Mob. Equipment of HQ & Batteries of 78th Bde. R.F.A. were inspected.	
	18th		General Routine.	
	19th		General Routine. Mob. Equipment of HQ & Batteries of 181st Bde R.F.A. were inspected.	
	20th		General Routine. Mob. Equipt. of 10th K.O.S.B. was inspected.	
	21st		General Routine. Mob. Equipt. of 224th Field C.R.E. was inspected.	

Army Form C. 2118.

WAR DIARY
or
INTELLIGENCE SUMMARY.
(Erase heading not required.)

May 1919.

Place	Date	Hour	Summary of Events and Information	Remarks and references to Appendices
On the Rhine	22nd		General Routine. Mob. Equipt. of Hqrs 6 & a/6 & a/7 a/Bde & A/6 a/7a Bde were inspected.	
	23		General Routine. Mob. Equipt of 6 - B. Bty 6 & A 7a Bde were inspected.	
	24		General Routine. Mob. Equipt of 151st Siege Bty R.G.A. was inspected.	
	25		General Routine. Nadir's Hill Sub Area Hqrs also Hqrs & 1st & 2nd Bde; 33rd Bn London Regt; 18th Mdt Regt; & 39th D.A.C., obtaining recruits for attachment to R.A.O.C.	
	26		General Routine.	
	27		General Routine. Wesden 16th Bn Mackedee Regt for Recruits as above also inspected. Reg. Equips of above Unit.	

Army Form C. 2118.

WAR DIARY
or
INTELLIGENCE SUMMARY.
(Erase heading not required.)

May 1919.

Place	Date	Hour	Summary of Events and Information	Remarks and references to Appendices
Lille Area	28th		General Routine. Inspected Regimental Equipt of 407 Bty 96 & 70 Bd.	
	29th		General Routine. Inspected Regimental Equipt of B Bty 47 Bd. R.G.A.	
	30th		General Routine. Collecting Ordnance stores from R.E. dump at Wolvelin preliminary arm to last Ed.	
	31st		General Routine. Inspected Regimental Eq of 460 47th Bd R.G.A. also "A"Bty + C Bty.	

Major
D.A.D.O.S, 14th Division.

www.ingramcontent.com/pod-product-compliance
Lightning Source LLC
Chambersburg PA
CBHW080858230426
43663CB00013B/2573